Servants of the Banquet

STORIES AND IDEAS ABOUT FIGHTING HUNGER

Cathy Butler

New Hope
Birmingham, Alabama

New Hope
P. O. Box 12065
Birmingham, Alabama 35202-2065

Cover design by Janell E. Young

Cover photos by Dan Bryan

Photo credits: Home Mission Board, pp. 2, 26, 32, 68, 70; Foreign Mission Board, pp. 20, 43, 45, 75; Brotherhood Commission, pp. 9, 10; Larry Burnette, pp. 50, 53; Jenny Quinn, pp. 57, 58; Ken Touchton, p. 77; Jackie Huber, p. 39; Arkansas Baptist Convention, pp. 63, 64

Dewey Decimal Classification: 261.8
Subject Headings: HUNGER
CHURCH AND SOCIAL PROBLEMS
MISSION ACTION

ISBN: 1-56309-101-1
N943118•0794•3M2

Dedication

To the memory of Charlotte Digges Moon, Southern Baptist missionary to China, a servant of the Lord who gave her life to help the starving.

"Then Jesus said to his host, 'When you give a luncheon or dinner, do not invite your friends, your brothers or relatives, or your rich neighbors; if you do, they may invite you back and so you will be repaid. But when you give a banquet, invite the poor, the crippled, the lame, the blind, and you will be blessed. Although they cannot repay you, you will be repaid at the resurrection of the righteous'" (Luke 14:12-14 NIV).

Foreword

" 'Then He will also say to those on His left, "Depart from Me, accursed ones, into the eternal fire which has been prepared for the devil and his angels; for I was hungry, and you gave Me nothing to eat; . . . Truly I say to you, to the extent that you did not do it to one of the least of these, you did not do it to Me" ' "
(Matt. 25:41-42,45 NASB).

I'm not writing this foreword as a former President, but as a Christian layman and the leader of the Carter Center, one of hundreds of private organizations trying to resolve the problem of hunger. Our Center's programs address those who are hungry in the small towns and inner cities of America and in the poorest nations on earth. We are free to try new ideas, and eager to cooperate with others. I am blessed with almost unequaled access to top leaders in the news media, in all nations and in the international community, and also unlimited opportunities to visit communities that are afflicted with poverty or disease. Despite these special advantages, our Center can make little progress when forced to work alone. The sad fact is that it has been very difficult for anyone to make much progress in actually improving lives of the desperately poor.

If not addressed, the afflictions feed on each other. We have several projects in African nations, and know that hungry people are more likely to start a civil war, which always causes even more people to starve. In the Sudan, Ethiopia, Burundi, and other countries, hundreds of thousands of people die in a single year, most from exposure and starvation. In fact, we have found that peace, freedom, democracy, human rights (including the right to food), and the alleviation of human suffering are inseparable.

The disturbing truth is that global per capita food production has steadily increased. There is more than enough food on earth to provide all human needs, and this will be true for the next 30 years. However, there have been few successes in alleviating hunger among the "least of these." In Africa, for instance, about 40 percent of the population are hungry, and the total number has almost doubled in the last 20 years and is still rising dramatically. In the Near East and Latin America the number of hungry people has remained about the same.

Numerous books have been written on this subject, and many hunger conferences held, some on a global scale. However, grandly stated goals are rarely met, and most new programs soon fade away or, perhaps worse, become lazy bureaucracies that just soak up scarce funding and qualified personnel.

Why these failures? How can the specific problem of hunger among the poorest people be overcome? Can poor government policies be voluntarily modified? Can technology be introduced without destroying the native culture? How can the importance of health and nutrition be emphasized? We must find the answers to these and many more questions.

This book is timely. Public interest in hunger has been waning because, globally, there is enough food. Inadequate attention is given to the critical problem of maldistribution of food either internationally or within nations.

There are too many uncoordinated, even competitive, programs within poor countries to produce more food and to distribute it fairly. Local people can't even understand what is offered. Such factors as soil fertility, government subsidy policies, the food distribution system, and imports of fertilizer and good seed need to be harmonized, both by private and government donors and within the needy country, involving official and private agencies and representatives of women, farmers, and environmentalists. This is difficult, but not impossible.

Servants of the Banquet describes some of the outstanding developmental work done by agricultural missionaries, but most missionaries and other private volunteers are not involved in comprehensive approaches to alleviating hunger, either in their conception or consummation. In any project, a top priority should be to develop the local family's ability to become self-sufficient in meeting their own needs. Program managers are moved around too frequently. I know of no country in which one person is responsible for the long-term success or failure of a nationwide project to reduce hunger.

We fail to realize that disease is still the greatest cause of malnutrition. Increased emphasis is needed on health and the impact of river blindness, guinea worm, and other parasites on the production and utilization of nutrients. Realizing that people can eat enough and still be malnourished, recent world conferences have emphasized the importance of such crucial dietary elements as vitamin A and iodine. The importance of this emphasis on health is demonstrated by the work of Sandy Shell Johnson in chapter 4, "The Great Carrot Experiment."

Deforestation has become the most critical issue in many poverty-stricken areas. It requires more and more time each day for a mother and her children to find enough wood for cooking, and in many communities the last trees are disappearing as more people seek fuel.

The domination of markets by rich nations is a cruel and often ignored affliction on starving people. Special price structures and trade arrangements cost poor countries at least six times as much as all the foreign aid that goes to them. Also, the export of surplus grains to developing countries tends to kill domestic food production.

Perhaps overriding all other issues in the long run is population growth. Even if a notable 2 percent annual increase in food production can be sustained in a country, continuing starvation is inevitable when a 3 percent growth in population is doubling the number of people every 20 years. Women must be educated, infant mortality must be lowered to convince parents they will have support in their old age, and birth control programs must be evolved and supported by political leaders. There must be some better coordinated worldwide approach to this highly emotional subject. Because of its political sensitivity, nongovernmental leaders might play a special role in a global family planning effort.

I have learned a lot from a missionary couple, who have solved a number of the problems outlined above. Jerome and Joann Ethredge, members of our Maranatha Baptist Church in Plains, Georgia, have been serving in Togo for more than 15 years. Jerome is an agricultural specialist, and has shared his knowledge with the farm families in a wide area around their home village. With the help of Baptist volunteers, he has constructed bridges across previously impassable streams, introduced new varieties of trees, and built dozens of ponds for irrigation and fish production. Jerome and Joann have demonstrated how food production can be greatly increased, stored better, and distributed fairly. Advice on health practices has ensured that nutrition is improved. All of this fine work, done as servants in the name of Christ, has resulted in a flood of believers who have accepted Him as Saviour.

Long discussions with the Ethredges have helped us at the Carter Center shape our own food programs. Let me be presumptuous and describe some of those efforts. In 1986 we launched a program to increase the quantity and quality of food grains in a few countries in Africa. Since then, we have had 150,000 farm families in this program in seven nations, including Togo. Whenever possible, we have combined programs in health, nutrition, and agriculture.

To expand the kind of programs the Ethredges have developed, we meet personally with the nation's president and the ministers of finance, transportation, agriculture, health, and education. We agree on the roles that we and the local government will play. On subsequent visits these officials visit the fields and testplots with us, and we give them maximum credit for successes.

Self-reliance is always emphasized. Habitually, we provide only one agricultural expert per country, while the government furnishes dozens of extension workers who are trained to work with assigned groups of farm families.

The poor people are directly involved and do more than any others to shape the final program in their village areas. We are concerned about employment, but we remember that a successful farmer has a good job. One Tanzanian farmer, who lives near the base of Mount Kilimanjaro, was proud of his harvest of 26 bags of maize, comparing it with his previous high yield of 6 or 7 bags on the same fields. He told me that his two sons, who had moved to Dar es Salaam to seek a doubtful livelihood, would now be returning to the farm.

We try to acknowledge the work and reliance of women in these programs, but I must admit that we are not always successful. In one country, for instance, I was invited to visit a master farmer, honored 2 successive years for his achievements. The entire village was assembled, his two plaques were prominently displayed, and he welcomed me in a shiny black suit. During lunch, served by his wife, I asked to visit his crops, and he reluctantly agreed. When we arrived at his superb field of corn, I asked him what variety he used. After some hesitation, he turned to his wife and learned the answer. The same procedure was followed concerning fertilizer, frequency of cultivation, and other questions. It was obvious that his wife had been the outstanding farmer, and that the award winner was only familiar with the family's few cattle.

We try to make minimal impact on the people's culture. Most families still plant their small crops with sharpened sticks and cultivate with hoes. Only as a community group are they likely to advance even to a few oxen for breaking land.

We introduce new methods, however, when appropriate, with the finest seed available, the planting of high numbers of plants in contour rows to control erosion, a moderate amount of the proper fertilizer, and adequate storage of harvested crops using local materials. In Ghana, we helped to introduce Quality Protein Maize, a high-yielding variety developed in Mexico that is tasty, has a good texture, and contains all the amino acids that are missing in all other corn. Hundreds of acres have now evolved from the few pounds first provided. It is our hope that these seeds will be distributed to all nations.

There have been some tangible results. On the average small farm, yields have been tripled. In Sudan, despite the ongoing war, wheat production was increased from 150,000 tons to 850,000 tons in the last 5 years. In Tanzania alone, 700 extension workers were trained, along with 50,000 farm families.

Despite these positive results, it is impossible to expand them appreciably or build on them without greater correlation of efforts with others. Hopefully, we can evolve a more effective way to alleviate hunger, using some of the principles already being demonstrated by the Ethredges in Togo and others outlined in this book.

Success or failure in reducing hunger, in our local communities or worldwide, will depend on the combined efforts of us all. This book will help to teach us how to follow the dramatic example of Christ—in providing bread and fish to those who hunger.

Jimmy Carter

Acknowledgments

How does one begin to say thank you to all the people involved in taking a book from idea to reality? Allow me to begin by thanking my husband, Larry. Some people assume that marriage to someone who's writing a book is glamorous or impressive. If I may be grammatically incorrect for a moment, let me say "It ain't no picnic." Let me also say that a supportive spouse is truly a gift from God.

Thanks also go to the staff of the following Southern Baptist agencies, who went the second mile in finding information and sources: the Home Mission Board, the Foreign Mission Board, the Christian Life Commission, and the Brotherhood Commission.

Through the years the employees at Woman's Missionary Union have been co-workers and friends, and they have applied their usual diligence to this project. I especially want to acknowledge Janell Young and Kathryne Solomon, who have worked quietly and steadfastly and who deserve more credit than I can give in just a few words.

I cannot fully express my admiration and respect for the volunteers, pastors, and missionaries who took time to answer questions and send information, sometimes from halfway around the world. Anyone can serve if he thinks it is in his own best interest. But only a person with a loving, willing spirit, who perseveres in heartbreaking circumstances, can be called a servant. Each person featured in this book has the right to that title. Each one expressed not only willingness but a deep sense of joy and appreciation for being called to serve in hunger relief ministries. I am left somewhat in awe of them all.

Finally, I offer my gratitude and adoration to Jesus Christ, my Saviour, Who has called each of us to the privilege of being servants of the banquet. I am thankful that He has allowed me to be a small part of this great endeavor.

Introduction

Servants of the Banquet is not a comprehensive study on hunger; other authors have written far better books to explain hunger than I could ever write. This book's purpose is to motivate you, challenge you, and touch you with the pain and degradation a hungry person suffers.

Hunger is not the star of this book, however, it is the villain—a lowly, skulking, evil, but very powerful, villain.

This book is really about the servants of God who say, "Yes, Lord, I will bring in the poor, the crippled, the maimed, and the blind and seat them at Your banquet. I will seek out the homeless woman in the streets, the migrant worker in the fields, the refugee, and the child. And I will do so with a grateful heart for making me Your servant."

Some people fear that hunger ministry is pure "social gospel," meaning that an evangelical witness is omitted. Every person in this book expressed a clear and firm goal of sharing Christ. For them there is no dichotomy of ministry and witness; nor do they use food as a bribe. They feed the hungry because they follow the example of their Master, Who filled every hunger He encountered.

Right now, imagine a long banquet table that represents the reality of hunger in our world. It's not a hard scene to picture. The rich sit at the head of the table, nibbling caviar and pheasant, while farther down the well-to-do gorge on beef and chicken, fresh bread, strawberries, asparagus, and chocolate. One guest is complaining that her fruit plate isn't fresh enough.

Beyond them sit the junk-food junkies. They brought their food from a drive-through window—Big Beefies, Mega Fries, milk shakes, and an assortment of chips and sodas. They aren't well nourished, but at least they will be full. Their motto is Eat 'til you drop.

The farther you go down the table, the poorer the quality

and quantity of food, until you reach the foot of the table, where a score of guests make do with rice and dirty water. They are at least more fortunate than the people who didn't even make it to the table. At a distance stand some who gaze longingly at the feast but dare not approach, for they are held at gunpoint by hostile soldiers.

But most horrific to behold are the people squatting at the feet of the diners, too weak to pull themselves up to the table. It doesn't matter—no one will make room for them anyway. Some beg scraps, while others quietly expire as guests look on nonchalantly. The dead bodies pile up in the background.

What an unappealing picture, you think as you banish the image from your mind. But it is more than an image; just as those pictures of starving Somalis and pinch-faced Appalachian children which we have grown accustomed to seeing are more than images. It is an expression of what we have, through apathy or ignorance or selfishness, allowed to be the reality of our world.

I hope the examples in this book will inspire you to envision and work for a new kind of banquet at which every man, woman, and child has a place. At that banquet no one is gobbling more than his or her share or begging the scraps others leave behind. Nor is anyone hoarding food or begrudging it to others. Everyone is laughing and happy, but none so happy as the servants who stand quietly in the background. Throughout the meal, guests who have eaten their fill rise to take their places among the servants, and new guests come to the table.

And every person knows Who has given the feast. Each one looks in loving gratitude to the Host at the table's head. Then, when the banquet ends, they bask in the joy of hearing His words: "Well done, my good and faithful servant."

May He be able to say the same of each of us.

Cathy Butler
Thanksgiving Day 1993

Contents

1

With the Dignity God Intended

Terry Moncrief, Atlanta

"Unless the Lord builds the house, its builders labor in vain. Unless the Lord watches over the city, the watchmen stand guard in vain" (Psalm 127:1 NIV).

Inner city.
Public housing project.

The words conjure up images of shabby rooms overflowing with neglected children, addicts slouching in doorways, and idle adults wandering sour-smelling halls. A place most people don't want to drive past, much less enter.

Yet thousands of people call the projects home. Some residents immerse themselves in drugs and violence, while others dream of the day when they can move away. Others just try to make the best home possible for their families.

However they view life in the projects, all the residents share something: they are people, and they want to be recognized and treated as such.

In Clark-Howell Techwood housing project, the oldest in America, one home missionary has spent more than 20 years doing just that. The work isn't easy. Dehumanizing forces surround him and his 200-plus volunteers. Terry Moncrief, however, doesn't speak of despair, but of good

Terry Moncrief and a young Techwood resident

overcoming evil, of light shining in darkness. He speaks of people as gifts.

"We don't see the people who come to us as interruptions, but as gifts of God. We see them as individuals, not stereotypes.

"Our goal is to see people empowered by Christ to break out of the cycle of poverty and learn to provide for their families," he says softly.

That cycle keeps turning in Techwood's 1,700 homes, where 9 of 10 families with children are headed by a single parent. Of those 9, 5 or 6 are on welfare.

Since food stamps meet only about half a family's food needs, a grocery ministry called the Master's Market plays a lead role in the Baptist center's ministry.

Ten to 20 families a day visit the market, which is open

two hours a day, four days a week. In keeping with their goal of treating people with respect, volunteers try to assist people quickly by sparing them long waits and check-ins. A family life counselor meets new people.

The families receive a food voucher equal to a certain amount of money and then choose the food they want, which is priced at about one-third of supermarket prices. No money changes hands, and the voucher allows some choice.

"We don't want to put people under a microscope," Terry says. "We want to treat them with the dignity God intended them to have."

Techwood residents respond to that dignity. Many are amazed at their first visit to the Master's Market; some leave with tears in their eyes. Accustomed to being processed through the system like a number, the respect and concern shown at the Master's Market takes them by surprise.

After visiting the Master's Market, families receive a home visit from volunteers, who pinpoint needs such as counseling or job training.

After 20 years at Techwood, Terry, his family, and his volunteers have earned the respect of the community. Most people know they are sincere and trustworthy. But some residents, such as Margaret, have a hard time accepting what the Techwood volunteers offer.

Margaret had three children, all by different fathers. She felt no qualms about asking for help. Striding into the center, her young face set in a mask of anger, voice vibrating with hostility, she would all but demand food. The volunteers never shunned her, even though they suspected she was selling some of the groceries to finance her drug habit.

Margaret expected to be scorned and she used her ferocity to hold people at bay. The workers, however, felt concern rather than scorn. But how could they convince her of that?

The question, What are we going to do with Margaret? bounced among Terry and the other workers.

Then two volunteers named Adele and Arthur told

Terry what they wanted to do. Adele was a Bible study leader. Arthur, a retired layman, had undergone his own transformation from a man who hated black people into a man who wanted to help people, no matter what their color.

"We have decided," they told Terry, "that we are going to love Margaret and let her know we love her, no matter what."

For 2 long years Arthur and Adele loved Margaret, not just in their hearts and thoughts, but with their words and deeds. She rebuffed them many times. But the walls of rage that Margaret built to keep herself safe finally crumbled under love's weight. The day came when Margaret and her boyfriend Larry became Christians.

Terry baptized them on a Sunday night. On Monday morning the couple appeared at the center again, marriage license in hand, and Terry had the joy of performing their wedding.

Years have passed. Margaret and Larry, now parents of a toddler, live five miles from Techwood, but still attend

---

It's not a sin to be poor. Some people are doing the best they can, and we help them. Some aren't doing the best they can, but we don't turn them away because of that. We help them because Jesus wants us to, and it's a way to show them Jesus' love."

—Terry Moncrief, home missionary,

Techwood Baptist Center, Atlanta

---

the church. Since they don't own a car and bus fare is costly, Terry picks them up for church.

As Margaret's life was once powered by rage, now it is energized by God's love.

"The whole family piles into the car asking questions about the day's Sunday School lesson or the Christian life," Terry says. Margaret's children learned the art of compassion well, and have already begun reaching out to their schoolmates. Had Adele and Arthur grown discouraged or disgusted with Margaret, the church would not have that vital family today.

Not every story ends like Margaret's. But Terry knows that judging on outward appearances is deceptive. He cannot judge what the Holy Spirit is doing in the depths of a person's heart, just as people outside a housing project can't glance in and know the mind and character of those living there. Serving the poor is a good way to learn wisdom and humility, according to Terry, who says, "To realize how many people don't have enough food to get by because the government systems have separated their families, because food stamps don't go far enough, because of sin, makes you think, 'There but for the grace of God go I.'"

Hunger and the Poor

- One out of 7 Americans lives in poverty.
- Senior adults and children account for 51 percent of the American poor.
- The average daily per-person welfare payment in the US is $4.00.
- Who gets food stamps? Over 90 percent of recipients are children, women, the disabled, and senior adults. The average award is $.50 per person per meal.
- More than 10,000 American children die every year from poverty-related causes.

(Facts provided by the Southern Baptist Home Mission Board.)

How Can I Serve?

- Contact your Baptist association or state convention office for the location of the Baptist center nearest you. Call the director or volunteer coordinator for information on how to be a volunteer. If you want to help, but aren't sure what you can do, call anyway. People who can love, listen, and treat others with dignity will always be needed somewhere.
- If you have skills in teaching or home economics, you can lead short classes on cooking, sewing, weight control, budgeting, thrift, food preservation, and nutrition.
- Offer to provide activities and companionship to children who wait at food pantries and shelters while their parents receive food and counseling. This gives children the attention they crave and allows the parent to give undivided attention to the counselor.
- Hold Vacation Bible School, Big A Club, and Backyard Bible Club in housing projects and low-income apartment complexes. Serve nutritious sack lunches and snacks instead of sugary drinks and cookies. Use the time to determine other ministry possibilities for the area.
- Deliver hot meals to the elderly and handicapped in housing projects. Check to see if such a program is already in existence. Most meal delivery programs limit service to the elderly. If this is the case in your area, start a similar program for the disabled who cannot cook or shop for themselves.
- Be an advocate in your community for job training programs, afterschool programs, and home health care that would allow the poor a chance to find adequate employment and break free from the cycle of poverty.
- Treat poor people with the same courtesy and respect you would anyone else. Let them know you neither scorn nor pity them. Before people can become self-reliant, they must feel some measure of self-respect.

2

Among a Proud People

Warren Hart, Kurdish refugees

"Do not forget to entertain strangers, for by so doing some people have entertained angels without knowing it. Remember those in prison as if you were their fellow prisoners, and those who are mistreated as if you yourselves were suffering'" (Heb. 13:2-3 NIV).

Delays, delays, and more delays. That summed up the first several days for the relief teams traveling to Iran to feed Kurdish refugees. Visa problems, mechanical problems, engine failure, the list went on. But now they had touched down in Iran, where hundreds of thousands of Kurds had fled in the wake of a failed rebellion against Saddam Hussein of Iraq.

Now the real work could begin!

But no, not yet. They discovered when they landed that the Tehran government had not yet informed the area governor that Americans were coming, so no clearances had been given, no preparations made. The first team had been taken to Dolenov refugee camp, but was forbidden to mingle with the Kurds. The second team wasn't even going to get that far. Warren Hart, associate director of missions for Bell Baptist Association in Texas, was a part of that team.

"Soldiers with guns searched our baggage, and we were taken to the hotel in Sanandaj," Warren remembered.

"Looking at it from their point of view," he explained,

"All they knew was a plane landed and out came Americans wanting to go work in refugee camps."

While the team rested, Jim Furgerson, at that time a staff member of the Brotherhood Commission, sought permission from the governor for them to work in the camp.

Unable to set up kitchens, feed the refugees, or even see the refugees, team members wondered, *What will this trip have been for if we don't get to do anything?* So the team did what they could do, which was to pray and pray again.

During the wait, Iranian Christian leaders arrived. They would help the Americans and oversee relief efforts after the teams left. By openly working with the Americans, the believers faced persecution and death.

Two of these leaders invited Warren on a tour of the city. All he really wanted was to find a bed and surrender to jetlag, but knowing that Middle Easterners are a proud people who hold hospitality in high regard, he said yes.

The next hours echoed the plane trip. Since he had never dreamed he would see Iran, he tried to take in all the sights. The number of people out at 10:00 P.M. surprised him. He also noted the gun-toting soldiers milling about.

For no apparent reason, the car began slowing. Soon he realized that his hosts weren't creeping along to give him a better view of the city. The car dragged itself to a halt. The two Iranians talked over the situation in their native language, while Warren sat still and prayed, "Lord, get us out of this." Though not afraid, he did want to get underway.

The number of curious bystanders coming up to inspect the car enhanced Warren's desire to expedite repairs. Whenever a soldier noticed him, Warren smiled reassuringly.

His hosts remedied the problem and they continued. Fatigue and stress wore on Warren. Passing a brightly lit carnival they asked, "Would you like some soft ice cream?"

Warren's exhausted body screamed, No! Tell them you want to go to sleep! When he spoke, however, the words

Kurdish mother and child

"Yes, thank you," were all that came out.

Hospitality is important here, he reminded himself.

Finally, at midnight, his hosts returned him to the hotel; and Warren fell into bed, thanking God for sleep.

The next days were no easier. Word came that the rice they bought was inedible. Jim Furgerson and the Iranian leaders visited the governor again, who bluntly told them to go away and work in some other area. A tea tray was brought in, with no cup for Jim Furgerson. The Iranian believers cringed; they knew a bad sign when they saw one.

As the situation became critical, the team met to pray again in one of the hotel rooms. After the prayer meeting, the men opened the door and came face-to-face with an Iranian soldier posted in the hallway. Things were looking worse by the minute.

Then, as swiftly as night becomes day, circumstances changed. Clearance finally came down from the Tehran government. The governor arranged for their travel to camp, and promised that he would personally ensure that any rice they bought was good. The bureaucratic roadblocks crumbled.

After much waiting and prayer, Warren's team reached the long, shallow valley where 14,000 Kurds lived. A dirt road ran through the valley; Iranian soldiers were everywhere.

The team began to taste refugee life. The Dolenov camp was in a high mountain valley where temperatures soared and fell, snow covered the high ground, and curtains of choking dust swirled around them. But the men knew they must endure it only a while; the Kurds did not have that assurance.

They set up camp on a Sunday afternoon, then rose early

Kurdish boy unloading relief truck

the next morning to prepare the cooking area. They dug holes for the poles, then unrolled the canvas covering that would protect the mobile kitchens. All the while, Kurdish men and boys stood as close as allowed, watching.

The Americans began to pull the canvas taut and as the covering rose, comprehension swept over the Kurds. Warren heard a voluble wave of "Aaahh!" rise over the spectators, who pushed over the road en masse to help.

"They were the hardest working people I have ever seen," Warren said. They were also proud, and the team wanted to handle feeding in such a way that no one was hurt or offended, and everyone was fed.

The pans they used were a potential problem—nice, sturdy, large metal pans for holding huge portions of rice and vegetables. They could give rice to a family leader, that person could deliver the rice, and then return the pan. But they had only a limited number of pans, and they imagined that a refugee woman would be loathe to turn loose of a nice cooking implement once she had it in her hands. How were they going to get back the pans?

They discussed it with the Kurds, and one man, an engineer, said, "Let me take care of this."

Kurd families were really clans of as many as 200 to 400 people. When a family leader came to collect rice, the engineer said, "If you want rice, you leave your passport with us. When we get the pan back, you get your passport."

The pans came back, and the first day the team fed 12,000 people. Unaccustomed to idleness, the Kurds jumped at the chance to help cook and clean. Their penchant for hard work showed up in many ways. The team heard reports that boys as young as six were fighting in the camps—over who got to go over and work with the Americans.

More than once Warren saw a supply truck pull up and Kurds line up to unload it. Ten-year-old boys were burdened with loads as large as a grown man would carry, and no one thought anything of it.

Since the Kurds began caring for the kitchens so quickly, Warren felt his presence wasn't required any longer, and he returned to Texas. He carried with him memories of a people he had never expected to see except on a television screen.

He also carried some sadness that he had not been able to talk with them about Jesus. As guests of a boldly Islamic people, their witness was general and low-key.

"If a Kurd asked why we had come we said, 'God was sad because you were refugees and God wanted us to come and help you.' Looking into the eyes of those children, I wanted so much to talk to them about God," Warren recalled.

Though few words could be spoken, the actions of the team touched the Kurds. When a religious leader came to visit, the camp leaders said of the feeding teams, "These are good men. They do not smoke, drink, or chase our women. These are good men." The leader anointed the hands of team members with rose oil.

Good men, indeed, both Iranian and American, risked safety and comfort to help a people the world had shunned.

Hunger and Refugees

- Over 16 million people in the world are considered refugees.
- With the fall of Communism, ethnic conflicts seem to have once again become the main force in generating refugee problems.
- While attention focuses on a few dramatic world conflicts, many thousands of people suffer from conflicts in the least developed countries. "It is these very countries that are most likely to respond to genuine Christian compassion as part of a holistic witness. Over 75 percent of the poorest and most neglected countries of the world lie in what we call World A."

  World A is that part of the world containing people who have had little opportunity to hear and respond to the gospel. One-fourth of the world's people reside in World A, which geographically is roughly the area of North Africa, through the Middle East and China, to Southeast Asia.

(Facts drawn from "Refugees . . . A Global Study on the Position and Places of 16,647,550 People" by the Research and Planning Office of the Foreign Mission Board, SBC.)

How Can I Serve?

- Contact the Prayer Strategy Office of the Foreign Mission Board for information on praying for an unreached people group, such as the Kurds. (See p. 93 for address.)
- Contact the Brotherhood Commission, Foreign Mission Board, Home Mission Board, and Woman's Missionary Union for short-term missions opportunities to minister among refugees. (See pp. 92–93 for addresses.)
- Most refugees who resettle in the United States will come with little knowledge of English or of American ways. Show a refugee woman how to shop at a supermarket or bake with flour. Teach her English so she can read food labels and directions on food packages. By teaching her to read, you also enable her to prepare nutritious meals for her family using American foods. Contact your associational office concerning English as a second language needs.
- Invite a refugee family to eat with you, especially a special meal such as Sunday lunch or Easter dinner. Such a meal might open the door to discuss why Christians pray before meals, what our holy days mean to our faith, etc.
- Before reaching out to ethnic or refugee groups, learn something about their beliefs and customs to avoid giving offense (see p. 94 for resources).

3

Where the Hunger Lurks

Jim Wilson, Appalachia

"If anyone has material possessions and sees his brother in need but has no pity on him, how can the love of God be in him? Dear children, let us not love with words or tongue but with actions and in truth" (1 John 3:17-18 NIV).

Drivers catch their breath when they glimpse the panoramic view from the mountaintop. The hills and hollows of Appalachia lie spread out below, the autumn colors settling over the land like some mountain woman's patchwork quilt flung across a bed in readiness for winter. Valleys narrow as knife cuts, where green deepens to black, intersect hills crowned with foliage in colors rich enough to shame a cathedral window.

"Beautiful," the tourists murmur. "What must it be like to live here?" they ask enviously as they drive away.

Appalachia deserves its reputation for beauty. But if the panoramic view narrowed and traveled downward into one of those green hollows, a different picture would emerge. The glowing fall colors obscure places like Hidden Valley, where shacks, privies, and muddy one-lane roads lie out of sight.

Just as the shacks can't easily be seen, neither can the hunger. Appalachia's poor don't starve; they live with creeping malnourishment that saps the strength from working men and gnaws at the minds of schoolchildren. Hunger peers out from the shadowed eyes of women prematurely aged, and flickers across the gaunt faces of the elderly.

In these mountains of east Tennessee, at Carson-Newman College, a group of servants have drawn together to feed and shelter those who have seen hunger face-to-face.

Jim Wilson, campus minister at Carson-Newman, directs Appalachian Outreach, which uses students, summer missionaries, local Christians, and missions groups in literacy, construction, and a variety of other projects. Denise Morgan directs Samaritan House, a rambling old home that serves as food pantry and shelter. Students live at the house, too, to assist the homeless who come there.

Mountain people lose their homes when they lose their jobs, when they can't live with family any longer, or when they take on the financial burden of a family too soon, according to Denise.

Some of the homeless have literally lost their houses. Faulty wiring, sparks from a wood stove, a candle falling into curtains—in old homes of dry boards, such things take only seconds to crackle into flames, and another family runs into the cold, lucky to escape with their lives.

Students at Sam House lead Bible studies and invite residents to church. Class projects benefit local people; WMU groups and student organizations hold food drives

---

Of course, the needs in the Third World are tremendous. But here in the States, there's a lot of similarity to that hunger, like absentee landlords that take resources and give back almost nothing. You don't see bloated stomachs; it's hidden poverty."—Jim Wilson, campus minister, Carson-Newman College

---

to stock the pantry. All this work touches the area people, but it also touches the students.

When middle-class students step out of their accustomed sphere to work with the poor, hunger in all its ugliness crawls out of hiding to stare them boldly in the face. For some students, the experience is like being confronted with a mythical monster they never really thought existed. They are not the same afterwards, Jim says.

The students try to plug holes in the social safety net wherever they find them. One such hole is training for the developmentally disabled, a service that has suffered from government cutbacks.

The students tried to help one young wife named Sally learn to prepare balanced meals.

"I cooked my husband a good meal," she proudly reported shortly after the lesson.

"Great! What did you make?" they asked.

"Potatoes," she said, and smiled. "Baked, boiled, fried, and mashed." It was a step in the right direction.

Small and careful are the steps taken to alleviate hunger and homelessness in the mountains. Working men and women forced to ask for help are embarrassed, and must be treated in such a way that they do not feel disgraced. After these families get back on their feet, some return to Sam House bearing gifts of food, repayment for help they received.

People born into the cycle of dependence need encouragement to break free of that cycle, but few do so. Denise Morgan estimates that of the 50 such families she has worked with, about 5 have really improved their circumstances. Change doesn't happen overnight.

Hunger is sometimes hard to see until you draw close to it. But the warmth and gratitude that blooms in a heart is sometimes hard to see, too, until you draw close. Jim Wilson saw it when he drew close to eight-year-old Bobby.

Bobby was a resident of Sam House. He had arrived with his mother. Every day as Jim watched Bobby step off the school bus, he would think how tough it must be on a child to stay at a shelter.

I bet the other kids give him a hard time. He probably hates being here, Jim thought.

Sam House fosters a family atmosphere, and residents do much of the cleaning and upkeep. One day Jim enlisted Bobby's help to fix the bathroom, a chore most eight-year-olds would not relish.

Bobby worked alongside Jim for a while, then suddenly said, "I'm glad to help you with this, Brother Wilson."

"Why?" Jim asked, a bit taken aback.

"Because," Bobby said, pausing to look up at Jim, "you've given my mom and me a home."

Hunger and Rural America

- As many as 500,000 homeless people live in rural America.
- Nineteen percent of country dwellers live in poverty.
- According to the 1990 US census figures, Southerners are more likely to be poor than residents of any other region of the country.
- One of 3 Americans is functionally illiterate.

How Can I Serve?

- Choose a home missionary in a rural area as your church's Christmas-in-August recipient. (Woman's Missionary Union magazines list names of missionaries.)
- Help fund a Jerusalem Project in a rural area. (For more information on Jerusalem Projects, see pp. 85–86.)
- This year, plan your church's missions trip to a rural area.
- Work with housing ministries such as Habitat for Humanity when they conduct projects in rural areas. This indirectly helps fight hunger; when people must spend an excessive percentage of their income to keep a roof over their heads, there is little money left over for food.
- Serve sack breakfasts to children in rural schools.
- Work in a literacy or tutoring program in a rural area.
- Make others aware that rural people are hungry too.

4

The Great Carrot Experiment

Sandy Shell Johnson, journeyman to Ethiopia

"The God who made the world and everything in it is the Lord of heaven and earth and does not live in temples built by hands. And he is not served by human hands, as if he needed anything, because he himself gives all men life and breath and everything else. From one man he made every nation of men, that they should inhabit the whole earth; and he determined the times set for them and the exact places where they should live. God did this so that men would seek him and perhaps reach out for him and find him, though he is not far from each one of us" (Acts 17:24-27 NIV).

Ethiopia has endured many famines in its long history, but none like the one that struck in the mid-1980s. Global media covered the tragedy in close-up, heartrending detail while the world watched, spellbound and horrified.

Then the famine ebbed, and so did the world's interest. The cameras and reporters went on to the next disaster. But a famine does not end the day rain comes or peace is declared. For long afterwards, the Ethiopians continued to bury their dead and pick up the pieces of their lives.

Although much of the world left, missionaries and volunteers remained to help the Ethiopians reclaim life.

This is the story of one journeyman nurse who remained to serve God, and in doing so learned that when human plans to serve God are thwarted, God is still at work.

In 1989 Sandy Shell came to the remote highland town of Meragna [Me-ran-ya] to teach health education to the Amharic people of the area. She hoped that improving diet and hygiene would help people recover faster from the lingering effects of the famine, and be healthier in the future.

Sandy took her job seriously. The people sat politely as she expounded on the importance of clean water. And how raptly they listened to discussions of malaria prevention!

After many such conversations, Sandy realized something. The people listened, but didn't do anything they discussed!

Back to the drawing board, she thought. Sandy spent months delving into acceptable ways to introduce change. But the Amhara had survived a killer famine; they lived in a culture millenia old. They weren't changing just on the word of a young female *ferengi* (Amharic for "foreigner").

As Sandy pondered how to work with the villagers, a dream began to take shape. She knew that xeropthalmia, or night blindness, plagued the rural highlands. Caused by severe vitamin A deficiency, xeropthalmia is discernible in the thick, milky, lusterless eyes of the sufferer.

Sandy particularly worried about the children. During the famine, children received vitamin A supplements, and night blindness decreased. But now the people were farming again and expected a good harvest. Vitamin A would not be distributed. Though nutritious, up-country crops lacked foods rich in vitamin A, and without a vitamin A source that the Amhara found palatable, night blindness would reoccur.

Sandy dreamed of introducing a new food to the up-country diet—carrots. A relief organization in Addis Ababa sent her 5 kilograms (11 pounds) of carrot seed. Those 11 pounds of seed could produce enough carrots to stock several supermarkets for a year, so it would certainly be enough for the local farm families—if they would eat a strange food.

The mission agriculturalist taught Sandy the basics of carrot farming, and they selected the village of Kewot as the project site. The village appointed six people to work as a health committee on the project.

Sandy and her good friend Frew [Frey-o] planned an array of activities to introduce carrots gradually. They mapped out discussions of the benefits of vitamin A and its presence in carrots. Ethiopian friends concocted recipes using carrots in traditional highland meals.

After all this work, Sandy hoped in eight or ten months to select some land and actually grow a batch of carrots. The people would begin eating them and the farmers would learn to harvest the seed for next year.

This is getting exciting! I'm finally going to see some results from my work here! she thought.

Her experiment was sidetracked by a coup attempt in the capital, which forced her to leave until things calmed down.

Less than a month later, Sandy was on her way back to Meragna via helicopter, the only way to reach the town

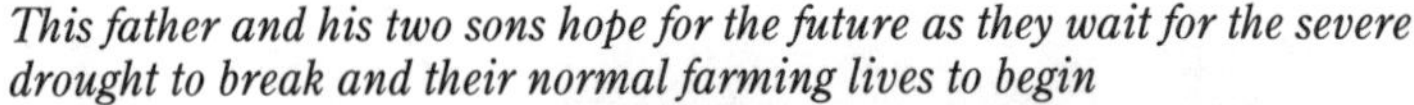
This father and his two sons hope for the future as they wait for the severe drought to break and their normal farming lives to begin

during rainy season. When she arrived, Frew and Higu, another friend, greeted her, bubbling with enthusiasm.

All this joy just because I'm back? I wasn't gone that long, Sandy thought.

The two could hardly wait to share their big news. They had gone to her house, found the seed, and planted a whole kilogram of it in Kewot!

Looking into her friends' joy-filled faces, Sandy didn't have the heart to tell them she hadn't meant to plant now, or that a kilogram was way too much for one village. She and Frew set out on horseback for Kewot. As her mount carried her over the rough terrain, she mulled over the whole situation. What would they do now?

Nourished by the rains, the carrot seedlings glimmered a tender green against the dark, rich soil. The patch, about twice the size of her own house and yard, lay on a gentle slope below a spring, and was surrounded by a stone wall. An around-the-clock guard protected the precious seedlings. Without her help or presence, the Ethiopians had begun the cure for night blindness.

"It's beautiful," she told Frew, and meant it. But silently she added, *Now if we can get people to eat them.*

Once again, politics disrupted Sandy's plans. Rebel soldiers were making their way to Meragna. Ethiopia had suffered the pangs of civil war for a quarter of a century, and now the pangs were increasing. Civil unrest and heavy rains kept Sandy away from Kewot, so the carrots missed the benefit of introductions and taste tests.

With rebels only half a day from Meragna, the missionaries were evacuated to Addis Ababa, where they heard reports of bombing raids over the villages. Returning seemed impossible, and Sandy was reassigned to a Nairobi clinic.

She thought her heart would break. Her friends had survived a famine. Now conditions were right for growing, but guns and bombs kept farmers from their fields. All the work the missionaries and believers had done together seemed lost. Frew's carrot patch—did it still exist?

What's going on here, God? she sometimes wondered.

At other times she could only rage, *This stupid, STUPID war!*

But later, Sandy saw that more was going on with her great carrot experiment than she had realized. Looking back on that time she wrote:

"Oh, but I had forgotten many things! I had left out the reason we were there in the first place, to share God's saving love. I had forgotten the resilience and intelligence of the Ethiopian people, and I had discounted the fact that Frew and Higu knew a great deal more about what would work in their culture than I did.

"I soon learned one of the greatest lessons I will ever learn. 'Watch, wait, and listen before you tell everyone how you are going to change the world. It saves a lot of time later when you find out what everyone else already knows: We serve the One Who is changing the world.'

"*I* left Meragna, but God did not."

Sandy heard that in the midst of fighting, up-country believers kept each other strong, and their peace was a witness to others. And in the midst of bombing raids, a bountiful carrot crop matured. The little green and orange vegetable became more than a cure for xeropthalmia. It became a symbol of God's provision in uncertain times.

While in Nairobi, Sandy received word from an Ethiopian worker who had returned to the highlands after the fighting calmed. When she heard the message, she could only marvel at the way God introduced vitamin A to the Ethiopian up-country.

The message said, "Tell Sandy that the people say her carrots are *batam teruno* (Amharic for 'very good')."

Hunger and Development Work

- Two billion people suffer from hidden hunger. They carry diseases caused by poor nutrition, which can lead to blindness, physical and mental retardation, weakness, and other disorders.
- Clean water is not available for at least 2.2 billion people in the world.
- Willingness and ability to do development work in Ethiopia enabled Southern Baptist missionaries to remain in the country when the Communists came to power.

How Can I Serve?

- ➪ Seek God's leading in the area of short-term missions. Could you go as an agriculturalist, nutritionist, or health care worker?
- ➪ Pray for development and agricultural missionaries to find culturally acceptable ways to teach and implement new techniques.
- ➪ Contact the Human Needs Department of the Southern Baptist Foreign Mission Board (see p. 93 for address and phone number) about funding a MANNA project. MANNA stands for Ministering Aid to Needy Nations Abroad, and is a way for individuals, groups, and churches to fund small, specific portions of larger hunger relief and development projects. (See pp. 85–86 for a fuller description of MANNA and how you can be a part of it.)

5

This Is Hard Work!

Disaster relief volunteers

"The Lord is close to the brokenhearted, and saves those who are crushed in spirit" (Psalm 34:18 NIV).

The year of Hurricane Andrew and Hurricane Iniki—1992. The year of the great March blizzard, the great Midwest floods, and the California brush fires—1993. And before and between the huge disasters came other floods, earthquakes, freezes, and tornadoes. Disaster rode across the country, streaming hunger and suffering behind it.

Sometimes on the eve of a disaster, sometimes in the wake of it, phones would ring in homes all over the country. Sleepers dragged themselves out of bed, workers took leave from factory and office, and retirees canceled vacation plans to answer the call to be disaster relief volunteers.

One volunteer who was used to answering the call was C. A. Easterling of Kentucky. After Hurricane Andrew flattened part of Florida, C. A. met other team members in London, Kentucky, where they set off for Florida together.

They faced trouble from the start. First a pin went out on the trailer, then the truck's transmission started acting up and finally went out, delaying them for 12 hours.

"Maybe we should turn back," some team members ventured.

"No, we shouldn't," C. A. insisted. "The reason we were called is still there waiting for us. Let's keep going."

On August 29 they reached Pembroke, Florida, and were briefed on their assignment. With no water or electricity, the team depended on bottled drinking water and their own generator. Sanitation became a big problem. The teams would usually dig pits to dump dirty water, but in Florida they struck shale about two feet down. They shelled out a large amount of money for septic tanks to be installed.

The disaster relief volunteers, 207 in all, served 328,864 meals during the days that followed. Cooks used number 10-sized cans of green beans and whole potatoes, carrots and corn, plus mountains of fruit, bread, chipped beef, corned beef hash, and cookies, washed down by gallons of beverages.

When they weren't feeding people, volunteers battled the muggy heat to do chain saw and cleanup work.

C. A. was no novice to disaster relief, but the aftermath of Andrew astounded him. When cleanup workers tried to reach their assigned areas, they found the maps were useless because road signs had been turned into just so much debris.

An area resident showed up at headquarters and said, "How can I help?"

"Come show us around," workers said. "We're getting lost!"

The hours were long and filled with work. Cooks rose at 4:30 A.M. Chain saw workers had to go out at 6:30 or 7:00 to get ahead of the enervating heat.

People who in one night lost homes and businesses appeared shell-shocked. Those who were indirectly affected by Andrew also suffered, but the strain showed on workers too who came again and again to what felt like their last strength and still found more hungry people, more work.

Emotions ran high, and sometimes domestic violence erupted as husbands and wives took out their frustration and rage on easy targets, each other or their children. At other times, survivors wept with gratitude that volunteers would come all the way to Florida just to help them. But many of the tears shed were in grief at having lost everything.

"Sometimes people would cry because they had nothing left and we'd say, 'Yes, but *you're* left, and that is what's important,'" C. A. recalled.

Reflecting on that experience he said, "You have to know some psychology and counseling to help these people."

C. A. found he needed diplomatic skills too.

"C. A.," a volunteer said, rushing up to him at the feeding station, "federal officers have been here wanting to know if anybody from that trailer park," the volunteer nodded toward what remained of a mobile-home park across from the station, "has been here asking for several meals at a time. They want us to refuse them food and report them. What should we do?"

"You feed anybody who shows up hungry," C. A. instructed. "And I'll talk to the officers." He knew the federal officers, looking for undocumented aliens, were

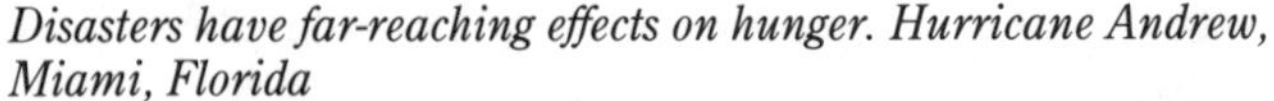

Disasters have far-reaching effects on hunger. Hurricane Andrew, Miami, Florida

hoping that hunger would drive them out of hiding.

"Now look," he told the officers when they returned, "if you want to observe who gets food, we won't get in your way. But we're not police, and we're not hunting undocumented aliens. We can't turn anybody away or turn them in.

"We came to feed people—regardless of who they are."

"OK," the officers agreed. "We can see your point." The men didn't press the issue, for which everyone was grateful.

The years of disaster relief have enriched C. A.'s life, and taught him some lessons. Once while cleaning up after a tornado, he noticed "a very dirty woman" hanging around, always at a distance.

"I confess I thought perhaps she was a prostitute looking for business, but I kept cleaning up, working my way to her a little at a time until I could get close enough to her to ask if she was hungry," C. A. recalled.

"No," the woman replied, then added, "well, yes, but I'm way too dirty to go up there," pointing to the feeding site.

"Come on," C. A. told her. "I'll guard the bathroom door while you go in and wash up." The woman gratefully followed.

It didn't take an expert to see that she was famished; but when C. A. tried to give her extra food, she refused.

"Oh, no," she protested. "Just give me enough for me and my husband. There's so many others hungry."

C. A.'s ears perked up. "Others?"

The woman pointed in the direction of where her house had been, and C. A. followed her over a hill to where 38 hungry people stood.

"It just goes to show," C. A. reflected, "you can get the wrong idea about people."

While Florida continued to dig out from under the hurricane, the Midwest began to fortify levees and evacuate towns as rain caused rivers to swell and levees to crumble.

Once again disaster relief volunteers, mobilized by the

Southern Baptist Brotherhood Commission, came ready to work. The Home Mission Board was helping in enlistment. One volunteer, Choice Watson, left South Carolina and his daily tasks as director of missions for North Spartan Baptist Association to work in Ste. Genevieve, Missouri.

Usually disaster relief volunteers are welcomed by those they serve. Ste. Genevieve, however, turned a cold shoulder.

What was wrong? Didn't they want help? Didn't they need it? Ste. Genevieve did need help, but the town was 80 to 95 percent Catholic, and townsfolk weren't sure how to take a bunch of Baptist rescuers. Besides, proud and self-reliant Midwesterners want to handle their own problems.

"We kept a low profile at first," Choice recalled. "Any witness was very low-key."

The team had their hands full with other matters as well. Floodwaters had seeped into the drinking water, making it unsafe, so a tanker was brought in. The health department placed tight restrictions on the feeding stations, a necessity due to rampant sanitation and sewage problems. The team borrowed tentage from the National Guard and set up big fans to disperse some of the humidity, which was so thick it sometimes made breathing hard work.

One thing the team didn't have a problem with was food. As the community tired, they accepted more help from the Baptists, and soon they were serving full meals. The Midwest is the heart of America's beef and grain industries so the food, especially meat, was bountiful and good.

The team continued to feed people and witness whenever they could. A Presbyterian woman in the town befriended them, and became quite taken with a gospel tract the team used. She asked for a quantity of them to distribute.

"That was pretty interesting," Choice Watson mused. "A Presbyterian woman passing out a Baptist tract in a Catholic town."

As with the Andrew relief efforts, workers began to tire in both body and mind. Watching people lose all their worldly possessions hurt. To strengthen their spirits, the team had a brief devotion before bed each night.

"You know," a volunteer blurted out at one of the devotions, "This is hard work! You couldn't pay me to work this hard. But I'll work this hard for Jesus." Other team members nodded agreement.

The rains beat down and the floodwaters rose inexorably. On a Wednesday night about two weeks after the team arrived, word spread that the levee wouldn't hold much longer. A request went out for volunteers to sandbag the levee.

Disaster team members donned their distinctive yellow hats and joined the work. As the rain poured down and the night deepened, onlookers and workers on the levee could still see a long line of yellow hats dipping and rising as workers passed sandbags along.

Morning came. The levee held. And Ste. Genevieve smiled upon her Baptist friends.

Several days later, when time came for the unit to return home, townspeople wept as they bid the Baptists good-bye.

Hunger and Disasters

- Natural disasters are not prejudiced; they strike without regard to race, creed, sex, or economic status. Many people who never dreamed they would be homeless or hungry are left with nothing after a disaster.
- One of the grave dangers after a flood has occurred is fouled water; sewage and other debris such as drowned animals may wash into the system, poisoning drinking water and spreading germs.
- Disasters have far-reaching effects on hunger. When food slated for community services must be rerouted to feed disaster victims, food pantries and soup kitchens all over the country may feel the pinch.

- Disasters are sometimes man-made and can be averted with better care of the ecosystem. For example, excessive cutting of forestland increases the runoff of rainwater, which causes floods. The cutting of trees in the foothills of the Himalaya Mountains created floods in Bangladesh which killed multitudes and destroyed crops.

How Can I Serve?

- ➪ Contact your state Brotherhood director to find out how your church or missions organization can be involved in disaster relief.
- ➪ Volunteer to go with a disaster relief team. Don't underestimate what you can do; if you can't wield a chain saw or drive a van, perhaps you could cook, counsel victims, run the office, or provide childcare. Contact your associational director of missions.
- ➪ Start a prayer ministry for the disaster relief workers from your church, association, and state. Ask for prayers during church services, start a prayer chain, or ask people to set aside blocks of time for private prayer. Keep abreast of what is happening in the disaster area in order to give people specific prayer requests. Report answers to prayer.
- ➪ Donate useful items such as cooking utensils, food, or tools to a disaster relief unit.
- ➪ Small children who have lived through a disaster may feel frightened and need something to comfort them. Ask the disaster relief team if they could use items such as stuffed animals or blankets to distribute to children.
- ➪ Join an ecology organization that seeks to protect land, water, and trees for use by future generations.

6

Without You, We Would Starve

Augustine Salazar, California

*"Blessed is he who is kind to the needy" (Prov. 14:21*b *NIV).*

The cool dawn breeze blew through the California camp. A few birds began to trill as the dark horizon turned gray, then shaded to ramparts of violet, coral, and blue. Golden needles of morning sun touched the cars and vans that sheltered sleeping migrant workers.

Families stirred in their makeshift quarters as the sun awakened them. Today was a big day, the day they signed up for housing at this government-subsidized migrant camp.

Just as other people camp out all night to be first in line for coveted tickets to concerts or football games, so these people were vying to be first in line for something they wanted desperately—decent housing.

If they missed housing here, they would have to live out the crop season in substandard private camps. A decent camp is worth the discomfort of sleeping by the roadside.

To them it is also worth enduring the hunger that rumbled through stomachs, and the thirst that squeezed the throats of children. By afternoon, little ones would be hanging on their parents, begging for food and water, but the weary adults would not dare lose their places in line.

Migrant children eventually learn they must do without things other children take for granted.

A worker stepped from his old van and stretched, filling his lungs with the cool air. He had stayed through the winter to prune the grapevines, work that ended the month before. Now he wondered what he could do through the early spring to feed his family.

As he took another deep breath he caught a whiff of something good. His mouth began to water. His empty stomach must be driving him to imagine things. Where would he find tacos, hot beans, and tortillas at this hour?

His little boy, who had crawled out of the back of the van, gave him the answer.

"Papa, look," he said, pointing across the road.

The worker turned, looked, and then looked again. In the open air, tables and chairs had been set up for dining, and women were dishing up the food he had smelled. He wondered what made them so happy. They were smiling and talking as if at a party. He would have been surprised to learn the smiling women had started cooking at 4:00 A.M.

"Papa, can we eat?" his son begged.

"We probably have to pay," he answered. Then he

Augustine Salazar talks with a migrant worker near Fresno, California

looked down at his hungry child and added, "But we'll go see."

Before they could reach the other side, they were greeted in Spanish by a kind looking man who invited them to bring the rest of the family. Other families were beginning to take places at the tables. A few people ate standing up.

"How much?" the worker asked.

"*Nada,*" the other man said. "Come and eat. The day will go easier for the children."

"Let me get my wife," the worker said, and hurried back to the van. In a few moments he returned with his wife and other children. The smiling cooks settled them at a table.

The kindly man who had greeted them watched from a distance as they savored each bite of food. Seeing their pleasure warmed him like the rays of the morning sun. Augustine Salazar, home missionary, took great joy in helping feed people.

He planned what he would say to the family before he went over to invite them to church. He could mention the children's Sunday morning breakfast during the winter. Just milk, oatmeal cookies, and orange juice, but hungry little mouths devoured it happily. He would also invite them to the upcoming Bible clubs and Vacation Bible School, where the children received oatmeal cookies and milk. There were so many ways to get nutritious foods to these people, if one tried. Thanks to Southern Baptist hunger funds, these ministries were in many such camps.

It's a real pleasure to feed the hungry."—Augustine Salazar, home missionary, California

---

Augustine approached the family as they were finishing. He smiled again. "Would you like to come to our church services? You are welcome there."

The man looked at his wife, and shook his head. "Thanks, but Sunday is our day to do laundry and things. You know, when there's work the hours are long . . ."

"Don't worry," Augustine said. "We have a service here in camp. The people asked us to come, and the manager says if we have insurance, we can come teach children the Bible."

The father rose from the table.

"We'd like that. And thank you for the breakfast."

"You can thank these folks from the Baptist church. They did all the work," Augustine replied. "They are farm families like you. They want to help."

As he watched the family take their place in line, Augustine thought of other families several miles away who were waiting for him to bring groceries. Even among the migrants, those families were needy. He recalled the last time they brought groceries to the front door of one family.

"Without you, we would starve," the father said as he took the food.

Augustine wondered if people appreciated the irony that those who spent their lives growing food were so often hungry. He also wondered if people who had never served the hungry had any idea of the blessing they were missing.

Hunger and Migrants

- In California alone almost 500,000 migrants traverse the state working in vineyards, orchards, and fields.
- Migrant workers often refuse to seek help from agencies because they fear deportation.
- Migrants with low literacy levels have difficulty finding out about resources and filling out forms to obtain help.
- Migrant children often have problems learning because they are too hungry to concentrate. Also, they may miss school to stay home and care for siblings so their parents can work, or because the family moves frequently.
- Sometimes two migrant families with four or five children each will share a house consisting of one bedroom, a bathroom, and a kitchen. Though against regulations, it is the only way many families can afford shelter.

How Can I Serve?

➪ Contact your association or state convention for names of people involved in migrant ministries in your area. Then contact those people to find out how they need your help.

➪ If there are no migrant camps in your vicinity, explore short-term ministries such as missions trips or Mission Service Corps involvement.

➪ Select a home missionary involved in migrant ministries as your church's Christmas-in-August recipient. (Woman's Missionary Union magazines list names of missionaries.)

7

No Such Thing as a Typical Day

Beverly Goss, Tulsa Baptist Women's Shelter

"The Spirit of the Lord is on me, because he has anointed me to preach good news to the poor. He has sent me to proclaim freedom for the prisoners and recovery of sight to the blind, to release the oppressed, to proclaim the year of the Lord's favor" (Luke 4:18-19 NIV).

Beverly Goss poked her head into the office where one of her volunteers was digging through a mound of correspondence.

"Hi, Jarene," she called.

Jarene Robison barely looked up. "Yes?"

Beverly displayed a letter. "A writer wants me to describe a typical day at the shelter. What should I say?"

Jarene retorted, "Say there's no such thing!"

Beverly, the shelter coordinator, laughed in agreement. "Well, could you try?" she persisted.

"OK," said Jarene, "as soon as I have a free minute."

After thinking a while, Jarene sat down to catch her breath and wrote the following "typical day" schedule.

9:00—Arrive, sack of towels in hand to aid with towel shortage. (Towels disappear quickly.)

Greet large number of women waiting for associational van to go to ministry center for clothing.

Help resident needing to contact other agencies.

Children request a video and are asked to wait.

Phone rings: Helpline calls for shelter count of 10 women and 15 children.

Office is a disaster because a resident has had a seizure and soiled floor and furniture.

Opened doors and windows to rid building of stench. (Unsafe because of neighborhood, but expedient.)

Answer telephone; uncover desk; give out medications kept in the office; sort mail; try to run some copies, but copier broken—again.

Prospective volunteer arrives for interview with staff member.

Call to arrange for carpet/upholstery cleaning (soiling from seizures; germs from resident with a positive tuberculosis test; stomach flu going around).

Call to locate a place for mentally ill resident.

Call ministry center to see if van is still coming. They are also shorthanded, and the van is at the associational office.

Arrange to get van while Mission Service Corps volunteer covers at shelter.

10:15—To associational office to get van, sign insurance papers to drive van, leave copy work to be done.

Pick up women and children to take to ministry center.

11:30—Trip back to shelter, then to associational office to return van and pick up copy work.

Stop to buy emergency groceries, get more disinfectant.

12:15—Arrive back at shelter to fix lunch.

Supply residents with bus tokens so they can get to Tulsa Housing Authority, job interviews, doctor's appointments.

Put groceries away. Refrigerator is crowded, and one is not working.

Call stores for best offer to replace refrigerator.

During lunch, carpet cleaners arrive.

Visitor arrives from Save Our Children to talk

with a pregnant woman.

Discover a bathroom lock won't work. Call volunteer to repair lock.

1:00—Back to office to type correspondence.

Phone interview with prospective resident. Can't accept her because she has teenaged sons.

Put on video for children; they have waited.

Complete correspondence.

3:00—Leave for home. Go by post office to deposit outgoing shelter mail.

Wonder: *Was Christ glorified in what I did or in what we provided? It's almost as though we're trying to cross a vast ocean in a small, overcrowded, leaky rowboat while bailing water with a tin can.*

Perhaps Jarene would not have wondered if she had witnessed the scene unfolding in Beverly's office. Beverly was chatting with a child who had just arrived at the shelter that afternoon with her mother and siblings.

Abruptly the child said, "Do you have anything we can eat? We're so hungry. We got up real early this morning and have been on the run from my father all day. All we've had was a little box of dry cereal."

Let nothing deter you from following our Lord's example. We must offer our loaves and fishes, and He will multiply our gifts to feed the hungry and relieve the poor. Get involved personally as an individual or family and pour out your hearts for the poor."—Ben Mitchell, Christian Life Commission staffer

---

In a few minutes the cook was serving a snack.

In a way, that scene is typical of life at the Tulsa Baptist Women's Shelter, where women and children usually arrive with only the clothes on their backs. The predictable events of life that provide at least a sense of stability, such as meals, jobs, church, and favorite TV programs, aren't realities for the homeless.

Whatever makes people homeless often continues to be their main source of insecurity even after they reach a shelter. Women on the run from violent husbands must keep moving. Other women are reentering society from prison, or mentally ill, or addicted. Some have lost jobs and homes because of a string of bad circumstances that dog them.

For all these women, life is one big uncertainty. Will they qualify for food stamps? Will the food stamps last? Will someone hire them? Will they ever again have a home?

Will they eat today?

For people who are "always on the edge of hunger," as Beverly describes them, being able to count on mealtime is important. At the Tulsa Baptist Women's Shelter the

Beverly Edwards, Mission Service Corps volunteer, tries to help a young mother learn to parent

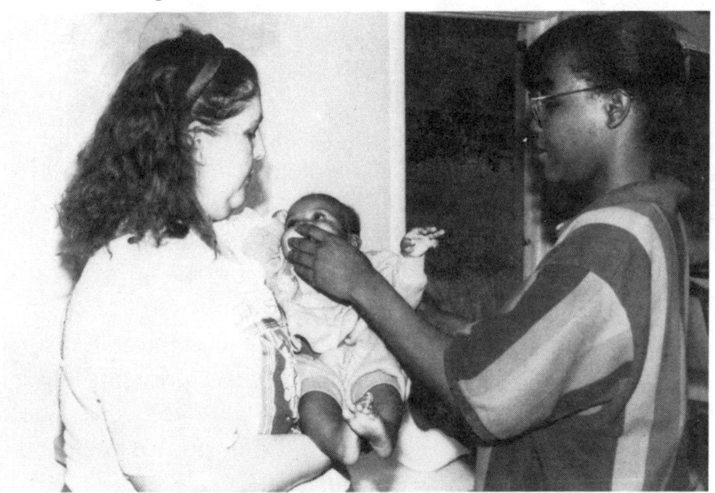

mothers and children are served first, then single residents and staff. Children gleefully ring the dinner bell.

"Hungry people tend to be greedy because they often do not know how long it will be between meals," Beverly says. Their food-fixation sometimes causes them to take way too much and either gorge themselves or waste food.

While that's undesirable, it also saddens Beverly to hear a scolding mother tell a child, "You've been bad so you can't eat." Hungry people see food as more than nourishment; to them, food is power, a power they sometimes misuse. Among all their other jobs, workers try to help mothers learn to parent their children without using hunger as a goad.

Shelter servants may never enjoy typical, predictable days. But the work they do in feeding and housing the lost and abused makes the shelter an island of stability in that sea of hunger and fear called *homelessness*.

Hunger and the Homeless

- Fifteen to 20 percent of the homeless are over 60 years old. "The elderly make up a large number of our shelter residents," says Beverly Goss. After a lifetime of working and raising families, most elderly people do not expect to end up hungry and alone.
- Between 2.5 and 5 million American elderly, most of them women, either go hungry or live on the edge of hunger. The high cost of medicine and housing leaves little money for food. The elderly often don't know what help is available, or are too proud to ask for it.
- The fastest growing segment among the homeless is unemployed persons and their families.
- Every night between 61,500 and 100,000 homeless children sleep in emergency shelters, welfare hotels, and abandoned buildings and cars.
- Single-parent families now account for approximately 34 percent of the homeless population.

How Can I Serve?

- ➪ Donate towels, linens, and other supplies to shelters for the homeless and for battered women. The less money needed for nonfood items, the more funds available for food.
- ➪ Volunteer to cook, serve food, or grocery shop for a shelter. One of the cooks at the Tulsa Baptist Women's Shelter is a Mission Service Corps volunteer.
- ➪ Offer a shelter the food left over from your church's Wednesday night supper. Volunteer to take the food to them.
- ➪ Offer to prepare special holiday meals or desserts.
- ➪ Check to see if the homeless shelter in your area has cards printed with the address and hours of the facility. Take some of the cards with you; when homeless people ask for money or food, you can direct them to the shelter. (Remember, if the shelter near you is for battered women, the location will be kept secret for safety reasons.)
- ➪ Take gift certificates to fast-food restaurants to give to homeless people who ask for money or food.

8

Tell Us, Where Is Hope?

William "Bill" Steele, Serbia, Slovenia, Croatia

"What good is it, my brothers, if a man claims to have faith but has no deeds? Can such faith save him? Suppose a brother or sister is without clothes and daily food. If one of you says to him, "Go, I wish you well; keep warm and well fed," but does nothing about his physical needs, what good is it? In the same way, faith by itself, if it is not accompanied by action, is dead'" (James 2:14-17 NIV).

As the taxi wound its way through the streets, Bill Steele sat in the backseat and stared out the window at what had been a gracious European city before the war. The taxi passed people digging in dumpsters. He hurt to think that these people stirring in the trash were likely doctors, lawyers, teachers, who once had nice homes and bright futures. That, too, had been before the war.

He tried to stretch his long legs, and sighed. He traveled constantly in his job as field coordinator for the Foreign Mission Board's relief work in the former country of Yugoslavia. Sometimes it felt like he lived inside a car.

The driver began talking about how difficult life was now. Bill liked to practice speaking Serbian, but he found that whether he talked to Croats, Serbs, or Slovenians, the topic was almost always bleak.

They chatted until the driver pulled the taxi to the curb. As Bill paid the fare the taxi driver said, "You know,

Missionaries Bill and Debbie Steele stroll outside the church where they serve in Belgrade, Serbia.

it just feels like there is no hope for us anymore. No hope at all." He drove away before Bill could answer.

As he turned to go to his appointment, the words rang in his ears. He heard them everywhere, on street corners, at feeding sites, in meetings. "Tell us, where is hope?" "We have no hope." "Do you see any hope for us?"

When he went to a Baptist church to deliver food parcels for distribution to refugees, he could give someone food and say, "God used Baptists in America to send you this food. God sent Jesus to give you life and hope." Those moments were some of the best he experienced in his job. When he had nothing to give and he looked into scared, desperate faces, the words of comfort sometimes stuck in his throat.

Hope. What a small word to carry so great a meaning. In this war-torn land, people lived on hope, and sometimes died without it.

What else, he wondered, could explain the phenomenon of retired people committing suicide? In one area 150 people had taken their own lives; they were not refugees or displaced persons, they just couldn't see a future any longer. Whenever he heard about another suicide, Bill thought of his own parents and grandparents. To come to the last years of your life and deem them not worth living . . .

The start of the meeting broke his reverie, and for the next several hours he worked on plans, projects, and strategies. His duties constantly changed, but right now

---

Don't take anything for granted, especially the food you're blessed with. Thank God for it and spread the good news around."

—Bill Steele, missionary to Eastern Europe

The real heroes of the civil war in dying Yugoslavia include Christians like layman Bratko Horvat (left), who pauses to examine relief supplies with Southern Baptist missionary Bill Steele (right) and Canadian Baptist mission official John Keith

he was providing school supplies for 130,000 refugee children in Serbia. Figuring out logistics for packaging and distributing a million notebooks and thousands of pencils was an exciting challenge.

Bill hated the fact that the war made people refugees, but he thanked God for allowing him to minister in this place and time. He loved giving people tangible expressions of God's care in the form of food and help sent by Christians in America. No matter how dark the days seemed, he could think of the hundreds of people accepting Christ at the church feeding stations, of the outstanding work the Slavic Christians were doing, and his heart was comforted.

And since his work with the Foreign Mission Board brought him into a relationship with the United Nations high commissioner for refugees, he was sometimes able to take a UN plane from Croatia to Serbia. Flying was a nice break from the constant driving.

The meeting went on to cover the use of Southern Baptist hunger funds to buy more food, the churches being used as feeding sites, and their relationship to the

Red Cross, who supplied them with lists of refugees needing food parcels.

They could have placed feeding sites almost anywhere and reached people, but by placing the sites in established churches, believers were there to witness and pray as well as give food. It was a good system.

The meeting broke up and he started home, happy that this trip didn't require him to stay overnight, as many of them did. Once home he greeted Vishnia, the young Bosnian woman who watched his children occasionally. After they exchanged pleasantries, she left and Bill got ready for dinner.

To Bill, Vishnia embodied the power of hope. She came to Slovenia from Bosnia because her diabetes and kidney problems required treatment she could not get at home. Her boyfriend in Bosnia abandoned her. Vishnia's brother had gone to Sweden as a refugee, and become a Christian. Knowing this, she decided to visit a Baptist church.

To the pastor she poured out her pain. "Pastor, I have nothing. Everything I have is given to me by someone else. I must have constant medical care, or I'll die; and I can't go home because they don't have the care I need.

"My life is empty and meaningless. I have no hope."

Gently, the pastor told her about Jesus, and Vishnia grasped Him as her hope in a troubled life. Bill and his wife, Debbie, had the joy of seeing her baptized, and now she made a little money helping with their children. Though her troubles had not disappeared, she could look to the future.

Dinnertime came and he sat down with Debbie and the children. Nine-year-old Berry talked about his baseball game, and little sister Sara giggled and laughed. When Bill cleared the dinner plates from the table, he didn't have to discard many leftovers. The Steeles didn't waste food. They had learned its value from people who didn't always know where their next meal might come from.

As he prepared for the next day's work, Bill thought again about how insecure the refugees were, how obsessed with food many of them had become. Food—its taste, smell, freshness, cost—seemed to prey upon their minds every moment of the day.

While he was thinking and shuffling papers on his desk, he heard a jangling sound and looked down to find he had dropped his keys on the floor. He bent to pick them up and holding them in his hand, remembered an incident some of the relief workers reported to him.

A refugee had been trying unsuccessfully to explain her plight to the workers. Distraught, she finally pulled some keys from her pocket.

"This is all I have left—keys to a house and a car that no longer exist," she said.

Looking down at the little bits of bright metal in his hand, he was touched by their symbolism. Wealthy people who used to have nice homes by the sea and two cars in the garage, and who never thought they would go hungry, suddenly have nothing to call their own except sets of keys that don't unlock anything anymore.

His administrative work didn't allow him the time to talk with the refugees and give food like other relief workers, and he missed the personal contact. But when he heard such stories, he understood why the workers cried after a day with the refugees.

Debbie glanced into the room. "You look like you're a million miles away."

"Sorry. My mind's been all over the place today," Bill answered.

"Daydreaming?"

"Thinking how good it will be when there's peace, and the markets are full of food again, and the refugees aren't refugees anymore."

Debbie took his hand and said, "But then you'll be out of a job."

"I hope so," he said, and they both smiled.

Hunger and Refugees

- By the end of 1991, there were 557,000 displaced and 58,000 refugees from Yugoslavia who had moved to Hungary, Austria, and Italy. Of the displaced, 300,000 are Croatians and 134,000 are Serbian.
- In Belgrade, about 81,000 Serbs from Croatia have taken refuge. Many of their towns are so devastated that those displaced have no home to which to return.
- The World Refugee Survey 1992 indicates that North America and Europe have 677,700 refugees and asylum seekers. This compares to 9,820,950 in the Middle East and South Asia; 5,340,800 in Africa; 688,500 in East Asia and the Pacific; and 119,600 in the Caribbean and Latin America.

(Above facts drawn from "Refugees . . . A Global Study on the Position and Places of 16,647,550 People" by the Research and Planning Office of the Foreign Mission Board, SBC.)

How Can I Serve?

- Give to the World Hunger Offering, which provides many of the funds for the food Bill Steele distributes.
- When you hear of wars and civil disturbances, stop and pray for the innocent people hurt by this sin.
- Pray at every meal. When you thank God for the food He has provided, remember to intercede for the many refugees and war victims who are hungry.
- Do not waste food. While it is true that you cannot ship your leftover mashed potatoes and biscuits to Slovenia, you can save money on your grocery bill by being a better steward of the food you buy and prepare. Use that extra money to help feed the hungry. Remember that when Jesus fed the 5,000, He commanded that the leftovers be gathered up "that nothing be wasted" (John 6:12).
- Look for ways to minister to refugees in your area. (See chap. 2, p. 13, for more ideas on how to do this.)

9

A Church Full of Ministers

Tim Cox, Memphis

"Jesus looked at them and said, 'With man this is impossible, but not with God; all things are possible with God'" (Mark 10:27 NIV).

"You want to start a what?" Tim Cox asked his congregation.

"We feel God wants us to start an emergency food ministry," they said.

Tim weighed the possibility. Attendance at Brinkley Heights Baptist Church ran 15 on Sunday morning. Members struggled to pay their bills and their little church building needed lots of work. But right across the road was the Department of Human Services (DHS), where members could see a parade of needy and neglected people pass by. Brinkley Heights had the location, the spirit, and the call for ministry—they just didn't have the money.

They talked, prayed, and decided they must obey God, money or no money. They set up shelves in a little room on the lower floor of the church, and held a food drive which filled about one shelf with canned goods. Tim applied for Home Mission Board hunger funds, and help from sister churches augmented those donations. Most importantly, the sister churches furnished eager, hard-working volunteers. In faith that God would supply, the church made itself available to DHS.

Tim Cox, pastor of Brinkley Heights Baptist Church, Memphis

Any fears Tim had about working with a government agency abated as he saw their relationship grow and strengthen. The agency screened applicants, then gave them a food voucher and sent them across the street to the church. This worked well, until DHS budget cuts eliminated the screening staff.

A new procedure called for DHS clients to go to another office several miles away to receive a voucher, then go all the way back to the church for food. Since many clients walked, they arrived at the church footsore and weary, often with pitifully hungry children in tow.

"There's got to be a better way," volunteers said, and asked to do the screening. The agency readily agreed.

In the beginning the church helped 6 to 8 families a week. Then they began to work with the Metropolitan Interfaith Association (MIFA), made up of churches of many faiths. Using a computer network, the church identifies each recipient by Social Security number, which helps ensure resources go to the people who need them the most. Even after linking up with MIFA, the church doesn't reject anyone; they give them the usual three-day supply of food. But if they are identified as frequent assistance seekers, the church refers them to long-term help.

"Referral is a big part of this ministry," Tim explains.

Soon the pantry was reaching 35 or 40 families a week. Church attendance grew to 40 or 45 on Sunday morning.

One Sunday morning a woman greeted Tim with a smile. "Remember me?" she asked.

"Sure I do," he said, recognizing her as a food pantry client from several weeks ago.

"I'm Karen. My husband's got a job now, and we have a place to stay," she said. "I told myself when I left the food pantry that when we got a place, we were coming to this church. Here I am!"

That Sunday Karen did more than visit; she became a Christian. Later the same day she stepped into Tim's office saying, "I think God wants me to work in that emergency food ministry."

Though thrilled at her spiritual rebirth and touched by

her eagerness, Tim hesitated to put such a new believer to work in a ministry which included counseling and praying with unsaved and troubled people.

"We'll talk about it," he evaded.

The next Sunday Karen persisted. "When do I go to work?"

"Come Tuesday and we'll talk about it," Tim said. When she arrived, he asked her to bag groceries and stock shelves. She worked hard in the tiny pantry, and loved it.

That afternoon another young woman, named Donna, showed up at the emergency food ministry. Tim happened to be the volunteer who talked and prayed with her. As they finished talking, Karen entered the room carrying bags of food.

"Let me take them out," she said; and as Tim trailed along behind the two women on the way to Donna's car, he heard Karen speak.

"I want to tell you what happened to me," she began. "I came here just like you did and saw that these people had something. I came back to church and realized Jesus was what I needed and asked Him into my heart. It's the most special thing that ever happened to me. It's what I was lacking."

Donna burst into tears. "That's what I need to hear. My husband's been beating us and threatening to kill us. I've

---

You can't wait on your pastor to do it. Our churches are full of ministers—you don't have to be ordained or go to seminary or be a deacon to do ministry."—Tim Cox, pastor, Brinkley Heights Baptist Church, Memphis

---

Tim Cox displays the food his church distributes to the hungry

left him. He doesn't know where we are; I was afraid he'd kill us if he found us."

Karen, her own eyes filled with tears, embraced Donna.

Tim said of that moment: "It was the most beautiful thing I've ever seen, and it didn't come from a pastor or trained counselor. God taught me a valuable lesson that day."

Later, they couldn't find Donna at the address she had given them. She had moved on in her quest for safety.

Karen, however, settled right into her new church home. She brought her husband and children, her brother-in-law and her children's friends, and people from the trailer park where she lived. A number of her visitors became Christians; and through her, the church began a Big A Club and other contacts in the trailer park.

One day several months after Karen joined the church, she came to Tim's office crying.

"Things are going bad for us, Brother Tim," she admitted. Distracted by upcoming work, Tim prayed with her and promised to visit later. A day slipped by, then more days, before he finally found time to visit Karen. He arrived to find an empty trailer. The family was gone.

Heartsick, Tim went to the park manager seeking answers.

"I'm sorry," the manager told him. "Her husband lost his job and started drinking, and well, they got behind on the rent. We had no choice but to evict them."

Tim drove back to his office, the words of a parable echoing through his mind. *There were 99 sheep safe in the fold. . . . Come, for I have found my sheep that was lost.* He sat in his office and cried.

Unlike Donna, Karen's family didn't vanish; but when church members found them the unemployment and drinking had already taken a toll. Sometimes the children visit church, and the church reaches out to the whole family. The congregation knows that with God anything is possible.

Tim, the pastor in a church full of ministers, said of that experience, "We all learned that we need to be better listeners when somebody says they are having trouble. We are still learning, and rejoice in the victories God gives us."

Hunger and the Urban Poor

- Ten thousand American children die each year because of poverty.
- One of every 5 American children lives in poverty. One in 4 American children under the age of 12 lacks basic nutritional needs.
- In the last ten years, more than 2 million American children became poor, while the number of billionaires grew fivefold.
- An estimated 20 million US citizens lack food for two or more days per month.
- A person working full-time, year-round at minimum wage still falls below the poverty line.

(Above facts provided by the Southern Baptist Home Mission Board.)

How Can I Serve?

- Organize a food drive to stock food pantries. Ask the pantry director what food stuffs they need. If you do not know what to donate, limit collections to nutritious non-perishables: peanut butter, rice, flour, dry beans, oatmeal, and pasta fall into that category.
- Collect grocery sacks for use at a food pantry. If the director agrees, write short Bible verses on the outside of the bags. People may not read Scripture portions placed inside bags, but they will likely notice colorful drawings and lettering on the bags themselves. This could be a good project for children's organizations.
- Volunteer at a food pantry as a receptionist, food sorter, bagger, or greeter. The way people are treated when they come to the food pantry is in itself a strong Christian witness. People facing unemployment, illness, or chronic hopelessness need to feel noticed as people, not numbers to be processed. You can be the one to convey the message that Jesus loves them, and hope that they will not always be stuck in a downward spiral of poverty.

  Before people can change their circumstances, they need the encouragement of people who believe they can.
- Find wholesale sources of food for pantries and shelters. Many pantries with adequate funds to buy food have difficulty finding good cheap sources of staples. (See p. 87 for a discussion of why this is so. Also see p. 87 for a description of modern-day gleaning.)
- Be an advocate for decent housing in low-income areas.
- Work with residents of high-crime areas to develop crime prevention programs. People go hungry because they have their food stamps or grocery money stolen.
- Be a liaison between government agencies, churches, and the poor. Find out where there is unnecessary red tape and work to eliminate it so people who really need help can get it.
- Establish a food pantry in your association.

10

Invitation to Moscow

Project Brotherhood

"'Come, follow me,'" Jesus said, 'And I will make you fishers of men'" (Matt. 4:19 NIV).

Denny and Jenny Quinn huddled together, speaking in quiet tones, almost whispering. They had just received an unbelievable invitation, and were debating whether to accept. The reasons to decline were piling up.

"Three months is a long time. What about the house?"

"What about my job?"

"We can't afford the airfare."

"We don't speak Russian."

Under all their uncertainties lay the real question: Why would God choose them to go to Moscow for three months as project coordinators to distribute 550 tons of food with Project Brotherhood? Communism had just fallen; religious groups were pouring through Russia's newly opened doors. Surely there were others more qualified to go.

Knowing this invitation came from God, they had to be obedient. They identified the obstacles: Denny's job, the care of the house, and the airfare. In quick succession, each obstacle fell, almost before the Quinns had a chance to catch their breath. They learned anew that when God issues an invitation, He clears the way for acceptance.

The only thing still to be done was to tell Denny's parents. Whenever the couple went on a foreign missions trip, the elder Mr. Quinn questioned the need.

"Why go overseas when there are so many needs here?" he would ask. But this time after they explained the trip, the answer was different.

Mrs. Quinn murmured, "I'm 80 years old and can't make a trip like that, but I wish I could go." They looked at Dad Quinn, who sat quietly. He finally spoke.

"I'd like to help with your expenses."

All this affirmed for the Quinns that their decision had been the right one. Immediately their church planned a going-away shower, giving them everything from a multi-band radio to laundry detergent. After many preparations, they found themselves walking on Russian soil.

Their job was to pick up Russian volunteers each day and bag food at a warehouse. When they had a quantity of bags containing flour, lentils, rice, and cooking oil, they took the bags to many of the new Baptist missions that had been formed since the fall of Communism where they and other volunteers would distribute the food.

While some of the other American volunteers wanted to push the work from dawn until late evening, the Quinns preached moderation.

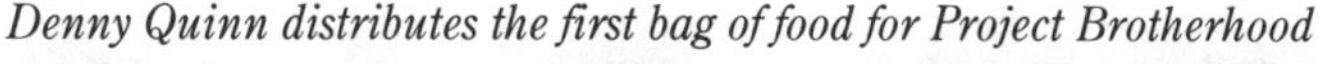

Denny Quinn distributes the first bag of food for Project Brotherhood

Baptist women in America made this cross that was given to a little Russian girl

"We're working with the Russian volunteers, and they have families here. They can't be so single-minded, and we can't last if we work too hard. Pace yourselves," they advised.

To fight off burnout, the Quinns toured the city and met as many Russians as they could. Many times their excursions opened the door to witness. Those impromptu visits are among the most touching of Jenny's Moscow memories.

"We gave an Eternal Life tract written in Russian and English to one old man who looked at it and said, 'I don't want to choose. OK, I'll choose hell. My life in Russia is hell, and it can't get any worse.'

"I thought of the parable of the rich man lifting up his eyes in the torments of hell, and I wanted to tell this man about hell and heaven and choosing Jesus." Jenny's voice filled with emotion as she recalled that day.

But joyful memories abound. They thrilled at worshiping at Central Baptist Church, a dynamic church filled with 2,000 believers each Sunday. Russian believers greet other believers of the same sex with a kiss on the lips, a custom extended to American visitors.

"Oh, Denny, I don't have words to describe receiving a kiss from a Russian sister in Christ," Jenny told him after their first service.

Denny, who had received a similar kiss from a Russian brother, was also speechless.

"Don't you have anything to say about it?" Jenny asked.

After a pause Denny said, "Yes. I have a new appreciation for razor burn!"

Jenny received other kisses. She and a young Russian believer named Michael went to distribute food in an apartment complex with many elderly residents. They knocked on one door a long time before an old woman answered.

Her eyes were red and sunken from pain, and a chair was her makeshift walker. Jenny handed her the bag while Michael explained their mission. The woman's joy turned to near ecstasy when she saw the silver can of cooking oil. Real cooking oil! It was like being given liquid gold. She grabbed Jenny and showered her with kisses as she wept.

Later, Jenny received a letter from the woman's daughter. It read, "I want to thank you for the parcel which my mother received from your convention. My mother is so old, she is 89, and she can't write, but I am writing for her.

"You do perform noble deeds by giving aid to helpless people."

As weeks passed, the Quinns became aware how a little bit, given in love, meant so much to the Russian people. They had suffered greatly, and smiles did not come to them quickly, but they were not ashamed to show their deepest feelings. Even a stick of gum merits tears, as one volunteer learned.

She met a man with three small children. Russian children love gum as much or more than American kids, so when she reached in her pocket and found three sticks of it, she presented them to the father. Through gestures, she indicated she would like his children to have them.

When the man saw the gum, he began to weep.

Startled, the volunteer called over an interpreter and said, "Find out what's wrong." The interpreter and father spoke for a few minutes.

"Just yesterday this man was in the market with his children," the interpreter began. "They saw some sticks of gum for sale, and the children asked, 'Daddy, can we have a stick of gum?' But this man had to tell his children he could not even give them a stick of gum.

"Last night he got on his knees and prayed to God for a way to be able to buy gum for his children. And today, he says, you have offered his children gum."

Tracts. Cooking oil. Gum. Such small things in a big task like Project Brotherhood. The Quinns are grateful God prepared those small things when He issued the invitation for them to distribute food in Moscow.

Spaceba is the Russian word for "thank you." When Denny and Jenny Quinn think of their time in Russia, their hearts whisper a prayer, "*Spaceba*, God, for Your invitation to Moscow."

Hunger and Moscow

- After the fall of Communism, Muscovites did not starve; but necessities are harder and harder to come by. The Quinns reported that one day 2,000 women lined up outside a church because they heard chicken legs were being distributed.
- The signs of hunger in Moscow were often subtle. Instead of looking for children with reddish hair and swollen bellies, the usual signs of malnutrition, the teams looked for women without fur hats. Women desperate for food would stand on street corners and in parks and try to sell their fur hats.
- Project Brotherhood was conducted under the guidance of the US Department of Agriculture, which required that each Baptist who received food bring a non-Baptist to receive food also.

"With this rule, even the government ensured that the Russian believers could do outreach," Jenny marveled. God was on mission.

How Can I Serve?

- ➩ Contact your state Brotherhood office, Woman's Missionary Union, or associational office to find out about missions opportunities such as Project Brotherhood.
- ➩ Provide financial support for a missions volunteer.
- ➩ Shower a volunteer with the many necessities for their ministry (add some extra treats for the family).
- ➩ Encourage your church, Brotherhood, or WMU to conduct a hunger relief trip this year, or add hunger relief to an upcoming trip.
- ➩ Go as a volunteer.
- ➩ Pray for missionaries.

11

When the Hungry Come to Church

Mississippi River Ministry

"He who is kind to the poor lends to the Lord, and he will reward him for what he has done" (Prov. 19:17 NIV).

The children piled into the van, rowdy, eager, clamoring for the driver's attention. Their ragged clothes covered bodies that were too thin, all angles and bones.

"We're havin' breakfast today, ain't we?" one boy asked, while his sister bellowed to be heard above him.

"What are we havin', Miz Treat?"

Rena Treat, taking her turn at driving one of Searcy County Baptist Church's vans, looked into the rearview mirror. She talked to passengers while she deftly maneuvered the van. Most of her riders weren't as poor as the Stone kids, but they all looked forward to Sunday breakfast.

"Oh, you know," she answered. "Bacon, sausage, eggs, biscuits, milk, fruit, just like usual."

"Hurray!" the children yelled, and began talking of other things. Rena thought again of the tragedy that in America, where food abounds and government assistance is available, these four children lived in a tent and slept on the ground. Most of the time, one boy told her, they ate cold cereal straight from the box because "Momma don't cook much."

She parked the van, and her riders piled out.

"Don't run, don't push," she called, and the children slowed just a fraction as they elbowed their way to the front of the line. Each child loaded two plates with food, sat down at a table, and practically inhaled breakfast.

Rena, the cooks, and the church members who ate together before early church service pretended not to notice when the youngest Stone girl wrapped up extra sausages and biscuits, then hid them in her pockets.

Searcy County Baptist Church has been serving breakfast every Sunday morning since 1988, when the church first opened its doors as a mission of First Baptist Church, Marshall, Arkansas. Started as a mission for people who felt uncomfortable in the more formal atmosphere of a First Church, the congregation had planned a pancake breakfast for the first Sunday. Now, five years later, the breakfast was a drawing card for the church. People liked the meal, just as they liked the church's informality—show up in blue jeans, have breakfast, and then worship in a church building that had once housed a car dealership.

As Rena ate she thought how much easier getting to early church was when you knew breakfast was waiting for you.

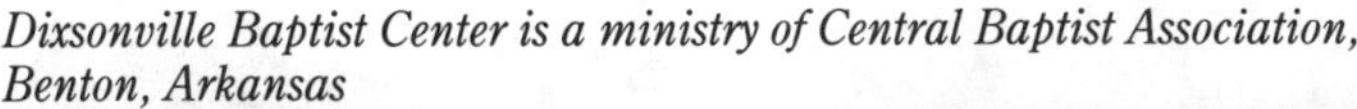

Dixsonville Baptist Center is a ministry of Central Baptist Association, Benton, Arkansas

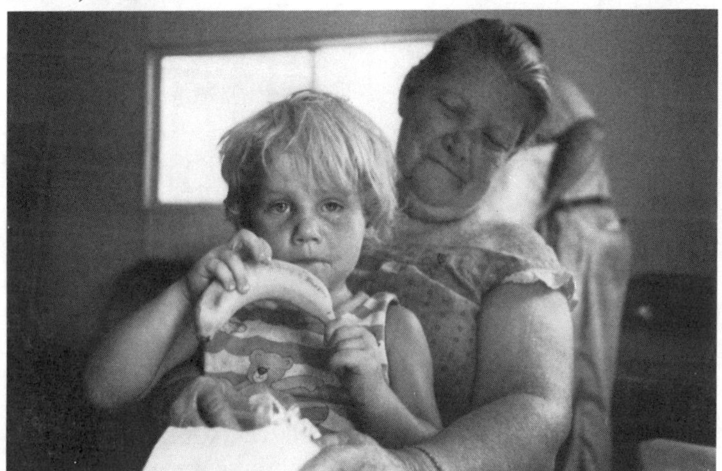

"Who knows when the hungry might come to church?" Arkansas is one of seven state conventions involved in the Mississippi River Ministry.

Another church member got Rena's attention, then inclined her head toward the Stone children. She spoke in low tones.

"How's the sister doing?" She referred to the oldest Stone daughter, away at college.

"Straight A's," Rena was happy to say.

"You know, those kids have got some potential," the woman replied, and Rena nodded agreement.

The talk of the oldest Stone daughter reminded her of

the day the young woman was baptized. All five children had become Christians through the church's ministry, but the parents would not allow any of them to be baptized.

When the oldest daughter turned 18, she said, "I'm of legal age now and can do what I choose. I choose to be baptized." And she was.

Rena looked around the room. The Sunday morning breakfast wasn't exactly a food ministry, but a fellowship time. While many people in rural Searcy County needed government help, such as food stamps, in order to get by, they didn't starve. Not many of the 75 or 85 diners came to Sunday morning breakfast out of hunger.

She glanced again at the Stone children, cheeks bulging with food as they ate, pockets bulging with hoarded biscuits and sausages for the times when "Momma don't cook much."

But then, she thought, *Who knows when the hungry might come to church?* As she bent her head to finish eating, she felt a glow of gratitude that when the hungry showed up at her church, the church was ready for them.

Hunger and the Mississippi Valley

- The Mississippi River Ministry is comprised of seven state conventions, the Home Mission Board, the Brotherhood Commission, and Woman's Missionary Union. The ministry encompasses seven states and 4.3 million people.
- In the 127 counties and parishes along the lower portion of the Mississippi River, living conditions are as follows:
  One out of 5 people live in poverty, as compared to 1 out of 7 nationwide.
  Almost half the people 25 years of age and older have no high school diploma.
  The infant mortality rate is the highest in the nation.
  Ratio of doctors and nurses per 1,000 population is the lowest in the nation.
  One out of every 3 families lives in substandard housing.

How Can I Serve?

- Find a way to bring clean water and sanitation to the most remote areas of the Mississippi River Ministry. Southern Baptists are well known for well drilling in other countries. You can do the same service here.
- Plan a missions trip to the area. Besides construction work and Vacation Bible School (VBS), offer a gardening class with free seed. Seek help from local county extension agents.
- Consider partnerships with churches in the area to find out what they need and how your church can assist them. Consider long-term projects as well as immediate physical needs.
- Agriculture is an important industry in the states of the Mississippi River Ministry area. Set up a network between agriculture professionals, such as wholesalers and successful farmers, and people who could raise some of their own food. Consider small efforts, such as beekeeping.
- Teach crafts to area women and set up a distribution system so they can sell their wares.
- Provide free or low-cost childcare for working parents.
- Provide transportation to the elderly who can't get into town to shop, buy medicine, etc. Or consider a grocery delivery service.
- Set up a co-op or farmer's market to promote sales of local farm produce instead of purchasing everything at chain grocery stores. This provides fresher food for the consumer, and boosts small farmer income.
- Consider any number of feeding programs listed in this book, such as milk at VBS, Sunday morning breakfasts, or a special holiday meal offered to the whole community.
- For more information about how to be a part of Mississippi River Ministry, write Tommy Goode, P. O. Box 552, Little Rock, AR 72203.

12

One Child at a Time

Ross Hanna, Arizona

"Let us not become weary in doing good, for at the proper time we will reap a harvest if we do not give up" (Gal. 6:9 NIV).

The Golden Corridor is the name gracing the part of Arizona which encompasses Tucson. Beauty, health, and leisure abound—for those who can afford it.

Home missionary Ross Hanna doesn't spend time rubbing elbows with the affluent who hold court in the Golden Corridor. Three ministry centers in inner-city Tucson, mission points and ministry centers in four border towns, and two Mexican orphanages keep him too busy for much else.

"You can't help the whole world," people glibly tell him, as if his daily struggle to feed people had not already taught him that hard lesson.

He doesn't let discouragers have the last word. "I know I can't feed everybody, but I can help feed somebody. One here and one there, and we're helping to feed our world."

Each ministry center distributes food and one center has a co-op that sells paper products and other necessities at low cost. Another center has started a church. But children remain the focus of much of Ross Hanna's efforts to feed his world. There is a program to supply formula to needy babies. And there is the food he takes to the orphanages in Mexico.

Ross Hanna, Tucson, Arizona

The children he helps don't know much about the Golden Corridor; their brief lives have been lived out in the shadowy alleys of ignorance and want. The mischief that sparkles in the eyes of most children never flickers in the eyes of these little ones; instead they stare out with dull faces on a world that neither acknowledges their existence nor provides for their needs.

But Ross Hanna and other servants see these children and they feed them, one child at a time. Sometimes servants must wait for a reward in heaven, but he received a reward on earth when his daughter and son-in-law went to Rancho Feliz, an orphanage he assists, and adopted a little girl.

"She's beautiful," he admits modestly.

But sometimes, even the most diligent and devoted servants show up too late. Through the Rancho Feliz orphanage, Hanna and some other workers found an 18-month-old baby, acutely malnourished. That small nameless baby died in the arms of the worker taking it to the hospital.

Every day many thousands of children like that baby also perish, after suffering a horrible and lonely death from starvation or fouled water or infection. They are not statistics on a chart; they are not lines on a graph. They are babies, meant to be cherished and loved and guarded, but who are instead thrown away like refuse, or sometimes quietly covered and placed in a corner to die by parents who cannot bear to watch their final gasps.

"You can't feed the whole world," spectators tell Ross Hanna as they watch him load food boxes, or apply for hunger funds, or take bread and formula to orphanages.

"I know," he says, not bothering to stop in his work, "but I can feed some of the world, one at a time."

Food assistance is an important ministry because people are hurting and hungry. Jesus must have thought it was an important ministry or He wouldn't have done it."

—Ross Hanna, home missionary, Arizona

Hunger and the World's Children

- By the year 2000, one-half of the world's population will be under age 21.
- Around the world, 40,000 children die every day from hunger-related causes.
- Over 177 million children have had their physical and mental abilities permanently damaged due to malnutrition. One-third of these children are less than 5 years old. These children will grow into adults who cannot reach their full potential and will need community resources to care for them—another hidden cost of hunger.

Children are the focus of much of Ross Hanna's efforts to feed his world

- By 1994 an estimated 145 million abandoned children lived on the streets of the world; and the number keeps growing.
- The world now holds 1.8 billion children under age 15. Of those children, 78 percent (1.4 billion) are growing up in non-Christian homes and communities.
- The world's children are exploited as slave laborers and prostitutes. Also, children are reportedly kidnapped and offered for sale to organ brokers for $1 million each, according to an April 1992 report to the Brazilian congress by Representative Celio de Castor.

(Facts supplied by the Human Needs Department, Foreign Mission Board.)

How Can I Serve?

- ➪ Give to the World Hunger Offering, the Lottie Moon Christmas Offering for Foreign Missions, and the Annie Armstrong Easter Offering for Home Missions, all of which fund ministries to youth and children.
- ➪ Encourage your youth group or missions organizations to conduct Vacation Bible Schools, Backyard Bible Clubs, and Big A Clubs in low-income areas. Bring interested children to church with you.
- ➪ Plan food ministries directed at children. Involve the children of your church or family so they will learn at an early age to help others. This may be an afterschool snack time, a Saturday brunch, or a lunch after church.
- ➪ Many churches distribute food baskets at Thanksgiving and Christmas, but people go hungry all year round. If your church or family already gives Christmas baskets, consider giving families picnic baskets or bags of staples at the beginning of summer to help feed children while they are not receiving school lunches.
- ➪ Keep a bank at your dinner table and allow your children to deposit loose change at each meal. Remind them this money is to help feed the hungry children in the world.
- ➪ Take your older children with you to volunteer at soup kitchens and food banks.
- ➪ Pray and seek counseling to determine if you should become a foster parent.
- ➪ Pray and seek counseling to determine if you should adopt a child. Many parentless children with racially mixed heritage, disabilities, or who are above preschool age are never placed in adoptive homes.

  (Adoption and foster parenting are deep commitments and should not be entered into lightly; however, if your spirit is burdened for the world's children, this may be God's calling for you.)
- ➪ Volunteer to work at your state Baptist children's home, a group home, or other institution for children.
- ➪ Donate food, clothing, and school supplies to shelters housing families.

13

Doers, Teachers, and Dreamers

Mindanao Baptist Rural Life Center

"'I have come that they might have life, and have it to the full'" (John 10:10 NIV).

Measles hits a Philippine village. After the epidemic, almost every family mourns a dead or blind child.

The epidemic strikes another village. But here, not one child dies. These children had been well nourished before contracting measles; and when taken ill, their mothers knew how to care for them. In this village a health care team funded by Southern Baptist hunger money had been teaching the people.

Jeff and Regina Palmer, missionaries assigned to the Mindanao Baptist Rural Life Center (MBRLC), had the joy of attending a baptismal service in a village where they had helped start a church. Afterwards the Palmers visited a church member to pray for his sick child. When the Palmers walked in, they found the tiny boy in the grip of pneumonia and dehydration.

They rushed him to a doctor, who assured them the baby would survive, but then said, "Had you waited one more day, this child would not have lived."

Starvation is not rampant among Filipinos, but the very young and the very old easily succumb to illnesses such as these because of chronic malnourishment. Lack of protein, a nutrient vital to strength and health, dogs most farm families. A farmer's life, already hard, becomes more burdensome when he is robbed of the strength he needs in order to work.

The staff of the MBRLC do everything they can to make malnutrition and illness just a bad memory for the Philippine farmer. The complete story of the MBRLC and the missionaries who staff it would fill a book. Director Harold Watson and his wife, Joyce, began the 50-acre demonstration farm in 1971 to help the poorest Philippine farmers. They saw that in a nation with millions of small farms (most only two to four acres) they could not go everywhere and do everything. Teaching the farmer to be self-sufficient was the key to development work.

The Watsons, along with the Palmers, Calvin and Margaret Fox, and Philippine staff, have devised ways to fight soil erosion, breed better animals, fertilize fields, improve seed stocks, plant trees, and protect the environment while doing so.

The programs that teach all these methods have long

God has truly blessed us as a denomination with resources that are far and wide. Yet if God blesses, there needs to be good stewardship along with the blessing. Will we stand before Him on the Judgment Day and say, 'When did we see you?' or will we hear Him saying to us, 'Come you who are blessed by my Father'"?

—Jeff Palmer, missionary to the Philippines

---

titles, so the staff uses initials when they speak of them. They sound as if they were talking in code when discussing the merits of SALT, BOOST, FAITH, and other acronyms. SALT (Sloping Agricultural Land Technology) and all its variations, BOOST (Baptist Outside of School Training), FAITH (Food Always in the Home), are all offshoots of the MBRLC's great strategy REDEEM (Research, Education, Development, Extension, Evangelism, and Mission.)

The MBRLC missionaries see the malnutrition and hunger of the people; but they also worry about the health of land. Overpopulation and poor farming practices sap strength from the soil just as hunger saps strength from the farmers.

Calling deforestation "Asia's number one enemy," Watson thinks that the Philippines may soon have the dubious distinction of being the first Asian country to lose its rain forests. Overzealous logging and slash-and-burn agriculture denude whole mountains. When the hard rains fall, no trees are left to save the land from erosion. The MBRLC staff want to help the farmers learn to help themselves, while protecting the land at the same time.

Agricultural missionaries are doers and teachers, but they are also dreamers. They dream of communities where children bloom with health, and women no longer grow old and bent from carrying water and firewood like beasts of burden. They dream of fertile soil and hillsides mantled with trees that sustain the land for generations to come. They dream of churches filled with believers.

We could feed most of the Asian countries with what America wastes."

—Harold Watson, missionary to the Philippines

Missionary Harold Watson, director of the MBRLC, chats with Warlito Lakiqugon, the assistant director

They also dream of what could be done in development work if all Christians opened their hearts to the hungry. While deeply grateful for the hunger funds and foreign missions offerings that fuel their programs, they see the need and potential for so much more. Harold Watson has traveled through much of Asia teaching farming techniques, and has seen the hunger and poverty.

"Christianity today lacks credibility around the world. Many people can't understand how we can talk about the love of God and our concern for people around the world and stand idly by while people suffer from malnutrition, poor health, and injustices. The poor and downtrodden of our world need help," he says.

Jeff Palmer echoed that belief.

"God has truly blessed us as a denomination with resources that are far and wide. Yet if God blesses, there needs to be good stewardship along with the blessing."

Recalling Matthew 25:34-46, he ponders what American Christians will say to the Lord on Judgment Day. Will we receive His blessings when He says, "As you did it to the least of these my brethren, you have done it unto me"; or will we be left standing there to say in confused disbelief, "Lord, when did we ever see you hungry?"

Hunger and Its Causes

- The hunger which prevents people from ever reaching their God-given potential usually does not come from flood or famine, but from underlying economic and environmental causes which can only be overcome through determination, awareness, sacrifice, and willingness to do justice.
- The root cause of unjust and oppressive economic systems and social practices is sin: greed, apathy, a love of ignorance, the embracing of violence and war.
- World hunger funds enable agricultural missionaries to teach small farmers how to overcome some of the causes of chronic hunger. In all this work, the gospel of Christ is preached and the love of God lifted up for all.

How Can I Serve?

➪ Work for policies that treat all people justly and provide for the weak and needy.

➪ Sponsor MANNA (Ministering Aid to Needy Nations Abroad) projects that promote health and agricultural education. Give to the World Hunger Offering. (See pp. 85-86 for information on MANNA projects.)

➪ In faith that people do not have to live condemned to hunger and misery, pray for missionaries such as the Watsons, Palmers, and Foxes and their work.

➪ Read and reread Matthew 25:34-46 and meditate on what Jesus will say to you. Govern your responses to the poor by this biblical yardstick.

Annual Fort Lauderdale Feast of Plenty sponsored by First Baptist Church, Fort Lauderdale, Florida

Hunger Myths, Hunger Facts

Myth 1 There is not enough food to go around.

Fact The world already produces enough grain for every person to consume 3,600 calories daily, far more than needed for sustenance. This does not count calories from all the other food groups, such as fruits and vegetables.

In America, 60 million tons of food is left in the fields or turned back at processing plants because there is an excess or because the food is not pretty enough to meet consumer standards. Restaurants throw out piles of leftovers, as do households.

Myth 2 Hunger is caused by natural disasters.

Fact While climatically created famines take a great toll, much hunger is caused by war, poverty due to unemployment or underemployment, environmental damage, and political or economic systems which oppress the poor.

For example, in many countries the bulk of land is owned by absentee landlords, and small farmers are tenants, much like sharecroppers in the southern United States. The landlords may dictate that the farmers grow cash crops such as cocoa or coffee for export. This enriches the landlord, but leaves the tenant with little to show for a year's labor, since his share of income from the crop will not be enough to buy food and other necessities.

Land which could produce an abundance of food instead produces little that is edible.

Myth 3 People go hungry because of overpopulation.

Fact The relationship between overpopulation and hunger is complex. Many families do have more children than they can care for. Those who live in violent and poor societies have many children in the hopes that some will live to adulthood.

The argument is often put forth that such families

should realize that having fewer children would increase their chances for survival. This is a hard argument to get across to many of these families. In many such societies disease is rampant, and crime and war are commonplace. There is no guarantee for these families that having fewer children will increase the chances of survival. Better medical care, sanitation, and peace, as well as food, help provide the security that children will survive.

While overpopulation does play a part in starvation, it does not adequately explain why so many American elderly go hungry, nor does it factor into the hunger caused by Hurricane Andrew or the floods of 1993.

Myth 4 Rural people don't go hungry.

Fact While many rural people are quite self-sufficient, others lack the know-how, the land, or the ability to grow all their own food. Hunting is seasonal; many fishing spots are now overfished, polluted, or closed to the public. As for gardening, the very old and the disabled can no longer do this. Many people own only the land their home sits on, or rent property which the owner will not allow to be gardened. The extremely poor lack utilities or running water, and therefore cannot freeze or preserve food.

(There are many ways to help rural people use the resources around them. See "Where to Go from Here" for ideas.)

Myth 5 Food stamps, WIC (supplemental feeding program for Women, Infants, and Children), and free school lunches are enough to feed people.

Fact Government assistance helps a great deal. But food stamp payments average only 50 cents per meal per person, and children do not eat school lunches when school is out. To provide good meals for 50 cents a person, a cook would need sophisticated skills in shopping, menu planning, and food preparation, skills which most of the poor lack.

Myth 6 Many people who seek assistance can't really be hungry because they don't appear malnourished. Some of them look downright overweight.

Fact Weight is not always a good indicator of a person's nutritional state. Poor people often rely on starchy, sugary, or greasy foods because they are cheap; however, since these foods are of the poorest quality, it takes more to quell hunger. A person can ingest too many calories and still lack vitamins, minerals, and protein.

Myth 7 There is no point in getting carried away in feeding the hungry because Jesus said the poor would be with us always.

Fact This is an especially dangerous myth because it uses the Scriptures as its rationale. While Jesus did say that the poor would be with us always, He also said that whenever we wished, we could do good for them (Mark 14:7). The Bible abounds with commands to feed the hungry, with blessings promised to the merciful servants who do so.

Where to Go from Here

No one can single-handedly stop hunger. No one can do everything. But everyone can and must do something to stem the tidal wave of hunger sweeping over our world.

No one denies the enormity of the task. The sheer masses of hungry people and the ever-mounting pleas for help are creating what Ben Mitchell of the Christian Life Commission termed "mendacity fatigue." People are tired of receiving a barrage of requests when they feel their gifts are but droplets falling into an ocean of need.

A labor organizer named Saul Alinsky once pointed out that when people feel powerless to change a situation, they stop thinking about it. Though he wrote from a secular context, Alinsky described the mind-set of many Christians when confronted with world hunger. Men and women of kind heart and tender sensibilities have ignored the problem because they feel powerless. It is too painful for them to think of thousands of children dying each day from malnutrition, of stunted minds and withered limbs, and of souls that slip daily into eternity never knowing there was a God that cared for them.

But we know that God, and we know He is not powerless. David Beckmann, president of Bread for the World, said in an interview with *Christian Century* magazine: "I don't see any power in the world other than the gospel's that can possibly move US politics in a direction that will reduce hunger around the world."[1]

We worship a God Who has called us to take His invitation to the poor. He would not issue such an invitation without planning to set the table.

So we cannot plead fatigue of giving, for "to whom much is given, much will be required." We cannot plead ignorance when hunger is on the city street corner, in the country, and on our TV screens. We cannot plead any excuse at all. What is a servant to do?

Pray

For yourself. Ask forgiveness for the times you failed to see the hungry as individual souls instead of some faceless social problem. Thank God for calling you to be a servant; then, ask God to show you your place at the banquet. Leave your prayertime with eyes open to new possibilities.

I know modern life seems to leave little time for ministry. While in the throes of finishing this book, sweating my deadline, I received a phone call from a woman who needed a favor. Could I please take her to the store so she could buy groceries and medicine for her sick child?

My first reaction was to say, "No, I can't take you to buy food. I'm busy writing a book on world hunger!"

Then the words of Terry Moncrief came to me: "We don't see the people who come to us as interruptions, but as gifts of God." As I left the house I asked forgiveness for not appreciating the gift God was sending me—the chance to help someone in Jesus' name.

For other servants. Intercede specifically for those who are teaching farming techniques, fighting desertification, feeding refugees, influencing policy, and doing all the other tasks God has called them to. Pray they will not grow weary in well doing, but press on in hope and joy.

For the powerful. Food distribution and nutrition classes are important, but changes on a great and far-reaching scale must be made before everyone is assured of daily bread. Pray that God would help the powerful of this earth to see their responsibility to the poor, and that justice would be done. This means different things in different societies, but we can pray that rulers and leaders would be endowed with wisdom, compassion, and faith.

For the hungry. Pray that those desperately seeking a better life will find it. For people caught up in the cycle of poverty and dependence, who can no longer even imagine any other life, ask for hope and courage to break free of that cycle. Pray for those who thought hunger would never happen to them, and are still dealing with the shock of their new reality.

Pray that all the hungry will find the ultimate hope, Jesus Christ.

Learn and Speak Up

Read the resources listed on pages 92-94. Listen to media reports on local and global hunger. While the command to feed the hungry is straightforward, the causes of hunger and the best way to help the hungry can be complex. Never settle for stereotypes and misinformation; always seek the truth.

Proverbs 31:8-9 (NIV) says, "Speak up for those who cannot speak for themselves, for the rights of all who are destitute. Speak up and judge fairly; defend the rights of the poor and needy."

Sometimes you will meet people who oppose helping the hungry, with reasons like this: There isn't enough food to go around; people bring their problems on themselves; you can't help everybody, etc.

When you hear these remarks, you can use your newfound information to give a different perspective. The person may be interested in what you have to say; but the person may become annoyed because he or she wants to hold that opinion, since they feel it excuses them from responsibility. I once saw a woman stomp out of the room when a speaker talked of helping the hungry. Another woman brushed off commandments to help the poor by saying, "Those don't count because the Bible says those who don't work shouldn't eat, and hungry people are just too lazy to work!"

Pray for wisdom, tact, and courage when discussing hunger with the unconvinced, the uncertain, and the uncaring.

You can also speak up on a public level. Bread for the World (see p. 92 for address) is a nonprofit organization that monitors and interprets public policy and legislation on hunger issues. Your senator and representative need your input on food stamps, taxes on food, WIC, school feeding programs, and other hunger issues.

When you write, be specific about your concerns, show that you are informed, and write in a spirit of Christian courtesy and compassion. Don't send anonymous letters; have the strength of conviction to sign your name.

Give Your Money

The World Hunger Offering. Giving to The Southern Baptist World Hunger Offering is an excellent channel for giving. None of the offering pays for administration or marketing. Eighty percent of the offering is used for overseas hunger relief and 20 percent for hunger relief in the US.

The Southern Baptist Convention observes World Hunger Day on the second Sunday of October. If your church does not already observe the day, talk to your pastor about doing so. A large portion of the World Hunger Offering is collected after World Hunger Day.

The Christian Life Commission has a number of resources (see p. 93) to help promote the day and to supply the latest information on hunger.

MANNA and Jerusalem Projects. Individuals and groups can fund a MANNA project overseas or a Jerusalem Project in the US. These projects are administered by the Southern Baptist mission boards and provide funds for food distribution, feeding programs, and development work. Many people featured in *Servants of the Banquet* receive funds through these projects. MANNA and Jerusalem projects allow people to feel more intimately involved in a certain work.

MANNA stands for Ministering Aid to Needy Nations

Abroad. Funds are already designated for MANNA projects; but when a donation is made to a MANNA project, the mission is notified of the sponsorship and the sponsor is credited with supporting that portion of the project. The amount donated will then be used in another area. This way, people can underwrite specific projects, but projects without sponsorship can still be conducted.

For example, MANNA funds go to Ladakh, in the Himalaya Mountains, to fund a development project which includes nutrition, preventive health care, agriculture training, and Christian teaching to the 30,000 people of the area.

MANNA projects teach people to use their own resources and manage their own projects with the goal of glorifying Christ and helping people become self-sufficient.

For more information, contact the Human Needs Ministries Office, Foreign Mission Board (address on p. 93).

"Jerusalem Projects are a select number of ministries throughout the United States which use Home Mission Board hunger funds to distribute food to the needy," writes HMB hunger consultant Nathan Porter. Sponsors can select a project in a certain part of the country, or a certain type of ministry, such as a shelter. Even small donations help.

For example, $30 will provide groceries to one needy family at the Rio Vista Center in Phoenix, Arizona. At the Clovis Brantley Center in New Orleans, just $1 will buy a meal for a homeless person.

For more information, contact Nathan Porter, 814 Canyon Oaks Road, Crawford, TX 76638-2720.

Give Yourself

Somewhere, perhaps near you, someone has a dream for extending the banquet table. The dream may be delivering hot meals, opening a food pantry, or teaching nutrition. The dream may be big, such as recovering some of the millions of tons of unharvested crops left in fields annually. Whatever it is, that person can't do it alone; he needs help. Or, perhaps you are the one to whom God has given the dream.

The ideas below are merely a beginning. Your own God-given creativity is your only limit in devising hunger ministries.

Gleaning

"When you reap the harvest of your land, do not reap to the very edges of your field or gather the gleanings of your harvest. Do not go over your vineyard a second time or pick up the grapes that have fallen. Leave them for the poor and the alien. I am the Lord your God" (Lev. 19:9-10 NIV).

Form an organization to collect discarded crops and distribute them to the hungry. Many farmers would be happy to know their excess is feeding the poor.

Gleaning involves more than permission to pick up the food; it requires a warehouse, trucks, boxes or bags, perhaps a forklift, and volunteers. In south Florida, one gleaning operation was given use of a building from the state, and local inmates boxed and sorted vegetables.

You may not know the difference between a hoe and a scythe; but even if you live in the city, you can still glean. Restaurants, wholesalers, supermarkets, even candy stores throw away tons of perfectly good food. If you know how to organize, drive a truck, sack vegetables, or know how to find people to do those things, you can be a gleaner.

Food Drives

Ask the director of your local food bank what items they need. While many banks can buy food from clearinghouses at a low rate (as little as 10 cents a pound sometimes) they may have little control over the selection. The food pantry can end up with shelves of hot sauce, candy, and sugar-free gelatin, but few staples. Churches and missions organizations can help ensure a balanced selection of food.

When conducting a food drive, remind people to bring the items listed. A food drive is not the time to clean out their own cabinets and get rid of odds and ends.

A food drive is a good time to involve children. Royal Ambassador groups hold races to collect canned goods, and conduct peanut butter-thons. Peanut butter is an excellent pantry food. Tasty, nutritious, and ready to eat, it is especially useful for those without stove or refrigerator.

If your church wants to do more than give food, look into providing a walk-in freezer for perishables, or adding a section of hygiene items and cleaning supplies.

Gardening

With help, even people in the inner city can grow some of their own food. Tomatoes and peppers will grow in pots, and other vegetables can be sown in wooden pallets filled with soil. Herbs flourish in windowsill gardens.

Work with local missionaries to set up small-scale gardening programs. Also contact your state's Fellowship of Baptist Agriculturalists, sponsored by the Brotherhood Commission. Include the county extension office in your projects. Their agents are trained to assist people in raising and preserving food, and the county extension office has a variety of literature available.

Meal Delivery

By delivering a hot meal once a weekday, and on Friday including two sack lunches for the weekend, a church or missions group can make sure a homebound person eats every day. Check to see if your area has a Meals on Wheels-type program, and if you can be a driver.

You may know of younger homebound people, such as the disabled, people ill with AIDS, or a pregnant woman confined to bed because of health problems. All of these people need meal and grocery deliveries also. If there is no such program in your area, perhaps you can start one.

Simplify Your Lifestyle

Some hunger advocates argue that changing personal lifestyle is a purely symbolic gesture. Others believe it is the first crucial step along the way to relieving hunger. You and your family will have to decide what lifestyle changes to make. Simplifying your life will free up more time and money to help others, and you may find that your stress level drops when you stop striving to keep up with the Joneses.

Don't waste food

This point bears repeating. At a restaurant that serves large portions, either take home a doggy bag or split the entree with someone. Don't take more than you can eat or heap your child's plate in order to tempt his or her appetite. Huge portions seldom entice a finicky eater.

Teach your children not to waste food. Do not use food for games or art activities; a child who fingerpaints with chocolate pudding will have a hard time understanding there are children who lack milk to drink. After all, if you can afford to play with the stuff, there must be plenty of it!

Weight-loss gurus tout the need to throw away leftovers. "Stuffing yourself won't help starving people in India," they argue. You may find that the best way to be a good steward and still maintain a healthy weight is to buy less food, cook less, and take smaller portions.

Eat low on the food chain

"There was a rich man who was dressed in purple and fine linen and lived in luxury every day. At his gate was laid a beggar named Lazarus, covered with sores and longing to eat what fell from the rich man's table" (Luke 16:19-21*a* NIV).

To people who live, and often die, on 250 calories a day, the American diet is luxuriously rich. Buying more vegetables and grain and less red meat, desserts, and junk food frees up money for world hunger and protects your body from some diet-related illnesses. Eat simply most days and splurge on occasion to enjoy rich food.

Fast

Fasting isn't to be done carelessly, since it can affect your health. People with certain health conditions should never fast, and healthy people should ask a doctor's guidance before undergoing a fast.

So why even talk about it? Fasting was an accepted spiritual discipline in the Bible. Some people have fasted for world hunger either by missing a meal and giving the money they saved to hunger causes, or to draw attention to the issue. Representative Tony Hall of Ohio fasted for 22 days to raise hunger awareness in Washington.

Hall, a Christian, chaired the Select Committee on Hunger, which was cut as part of a congressional budget-trimming effort. Hall felt the plight of the hungry was so horrendous, and the attitude of Congress so lackadaisical, that he had to take a drastic, very personal route to get some action. He ended his fast after the agriculture secretary promised to organize conferences on hunger.

Teach Others

Hunger will never end as long as hunger ministry is seen as a pet concern of a few people. Everyone must be involved; but before some will become involved, they need to know more about the problem.

Schedule a Bible study

Examine Christian Life Commission resources for Bible studies on hunger and set aside a time for study and discussion.

Talk about hunger at appropriate times

This means in Sunday School, as sermon illustrations, and as a prayer concern during prayer meeting. It does not mean turning to someone at a church party and saying, "I bet a lot of little starving kids would like to have that cake you're wolfing down." Making people feel guilty for having enough to eat is not the route you want to take.

Host a hunger meal

Hunger meals can be conducted several ways. Check the Brotherhood Commission's hunger manual (see resources) for directions. The point of the meal is to give people a new and personal perspective on what it is like to be the one going hungry in the midst of bounty. Order hunger awareness place mats from the Christian Life Commission to use for the meal, or make your own.

Network

As you have learned, hunger has many causes. Food distribution alone won't make hunger go away. By working with larger organizations, such as your association and state convention, WMU, and Brotherhood, you can do things one person or one church cannot do. You can strike at the causes of hunger, such as illiteracy, family instability, public policy, and environmental damage.

Contact Bread for the World (see p. 85). Also consider starting your own Bread for the World chapter or forming a hunger task force in your church which would work with all church programs.

---

[1]"The Politics of Hunger: An Interview with David Beckmann," *Christian Century,* April 28, 1993, 456.

Resources

Books

The Hunger Project. *Ending Hunger: An Idea Whose Time Has Come.* New York: Praeger Publishers, 1985.

Knapp, Doug, and Evelyn Knapp. *Thunder in the Valley.* Nashville: Broadman Press, 1986. This autobiography of an agricultural missionary couple depicts how agriculture and evangelism work together to change people's lives.

Sider, Ronald J. *Rich Christians in an Age of Hunger: A Biblical Study.* Rev. and expanded. Downers Grove: InterVarsity Press, 1984. A comprehensive look at the biblical basis for feeding the hungry and the Christian's responsibility to the hunger crisis.

Simon, Arthur. *Bread for the World.* Rev. and updated. Grand Rapids: Wm. B. Eerdmans Publishing Company, 1984. Examination of the underlying economic, physical, political, and spiritual causes of hunger and what to do about them.

Periodicals

Seeds, P. O. Box 6170, Waco, TX 76706. Subscription price: $20 for one year; $38 for two years. Biblically based magazine with articles and ideas on grassroots efforts to fight hunger.

Light, a free publication of the Christian Life Commission, which frequently carries articles on hunger (address follows).

Organizations

Bread for the World, 1100 Wayne Avenue, Suite 1000, Silver Springs, MD 20910; (301) 608-2400. Bread for the World does not directly distribute food or relief; it monitors legislation pertaining to hunger issues and alerts members to ways they can sway public policy in favor of the poor and hungry.

Denominational materials

Brotherhood Commission
1548 Poplar Avenue, Memphis, TN 38104-2493
Hunger: A Manual for Ministry, a manual for use by young men and adults.

Home Mission Board
1350 Spring Street, NW, Atlanta, GA 30367-5601
1 (800) 634-2462
Church and Community Needs Survey Guide (301-28F)
Poverty and Hunger in the United States (360-38F)
Beginning a Food Distribution Ministry (366-21F)
Beginning a Ministry with Migrant Workers (366-22FP)
Beginning Church Weekday Ministries (366-23FP)
How Your Church Can Minister with Homeless People (632-78FP)
Domestic Hunger (301-22P)

Foreign Mission Board
P. O. 6767, Richmond, VA 23230
1 (800) 866-3621
Volunteers in Human Needs (VIM–HUMAN)
In His Name: Human Needs Ministries (V–HUMANVHS)

Christian Life Commission
901 Commerce, Suite 550, Nashville, TN 37203-5266
(615) 244-2495
The Christian Life Commission has a large number of materials for promoting world hunger awareness in the church. Several resources apply directly to the World Hunger Offering and World Hunger Day in Southern Baptist churches. Posters, place mats, videotapes, a play script, stickers, pamphlets, calendars, and hunger guides are available.

Request a World Hunger Resources Order Form at the address and telephone number listed above.

Also request to receive *Light* (see p. 92).

Woman's Missionary Union
P. O. Box 830010
Birmingham, AL 35283-0010
(205) 991-4933

Bock, Betty. *You Can Make a Difference* (Birmingham, AL: Woman's Missionary Union, 1992). $6.95

Bolton, Joy. *Ideas for Community Ministries* (Birmingham, AL: Woman's Missionary Union, 1993). $5.95

Hunke, Dixie L. *Attitudes and Etiquette.* Birmingham, AL: New Hope, 1989. A primer on cross-cultural communications and relationships. $2.95

Marler, Malcolm. *Ideas for Homebound Ministries.* Birmingham, AL: New Hope, 1993. $4.95

"A Message of Love"; package of 25 self-stick Scripture portions which can be affixed to grocery bags, cans, and food packages. $1.95

Snowden, Mark et al. *Meeting the World.* Birmingham, AL: New Hope, 1992. A follow-up to *Attitudes and Etiquette.* Covers forming relationships with a variety of ethnic and religious groups. $3.95
(Both *Attitudes and Etiquette* and *Meeting the World* are excellent resources for preparation in working with refugees, migrants, and ethnic groups in the US.)

Ideas for Group Study

Before the study you will want to enlist someone to help gather data about hunger in your church's sphere of influence. Wherever your church is located, do not underestimate the probability that hungry or undernourished people live nearby.

When conducting the research, check with your Baptist association and the missions department of your state convention for existing ministries which you can support, and for new hunger ministries you can begin. You don't want to duplicate ministries, but neither do you want to oversupply one ministry while other needs go lacking.

If you live in an affluent area, some church members may scoff at the idea that hunger is a real local problem. Facts and statistics from home missionaries, directors of missions, and government agencies can enlighten skeptics and motivate more people to become involved.

Begin preparation by reading *Servants of the Banquet*. Focus on information you think the group has never heard, and on information that would apply to your situation.

Copy some of the quotes scattered throughout the book onto miniposters to place around the room during the study. Also copy "Hunger Myths, Hunger Facts" on pages 79-81 for each group member.

Order the denominational resources listed on pages 92-94. Practice good stewardship by ordering only what you need of the free items.

Invite the WMU and Brotherhood directors to be a part of the study; their organizations may already be involved in hunger relief projects or would like to learn more about them.

Encourage people to read *Servants of the Banquet* before the study, but do not make it a prerequisite. Some people will decide to read the book after the group has met.

If you want music, enlist someone to sing "The Servant Song" (*Baptist Hymnal*, 1991 edition) at the beginning of each study session and at the conclusion of the study.

Learning Activities

Activities 2 through 9 are suggestions. You may use them as they are described here or substitute other stories and activities which you feel are more appropriate for your group. However many of the following activities you choose to do, be sure to use activity 1 as an introduction and activity 10 as the conclusion.

1. Copy the following scenarios on index cards and give one card to each participant as the study begins. Ask participants to decide what they would do in that situation.

a) There is no food in the house; you have no money, no job, and nothing left to sell. Your child comes to you crying from hunger.

b) While you are sitting down to dinner, a frightened woman knocks on the door and calls out that she and her children haven't eaten in three days. She asks if you could help her.

c) It is time to contribute to the World Hunger Offering. You have saved a certain amount for the offering, but discover that something you've wanted for a long time has gone on sale for that same amount of money. You have no extra money at this time.

d) Someone from another country comes to live in your neighborhood. He wants to feed you a new type of food that will make you healthier. You've never seen this food before; he tells you to trust him because he is doing this out of love for you.

e) You have not eaten in days; your children are suffering from scurvy and night blindness due to lack of vitamins. You are sitting down together outside an expensive-looking house. Someone opens the door, and you look up, hoping for help. Instead, the person carries out a large amount of leftover food and throws it into the garbage. The person never looks at you.

f) Everything you own is wiped out in a natural disaster. All your friends and relatives are in the same situation. Stunned, you are wondering where to turn when someone calling himself a Brotherhood disaster relief volunteer offers you a hot meal.

Some of these scenarios confront the participant with what it's like to be a hungry person. Others challenge participants to think of their responses to the hungry. Invite discussion of how people felt when they read their scenario. Do not pass judgment on any response. The point of the activity is to start people thinking about hunger. If a participant indicates that a scenario would never apply to his life, tell the group that you will be learning about many people who thought they were immune to hunger, but learned differently. Emphasize that hunger doesn't just afflict other people. Hunger affects everyone—both those who suffer from it and those who have the means to alleviate it.

2. Distribute "Hunger Myths, Hunger Facts" to each participant. Which myths had they believed to be true? What surprised them the most?

3. Before the study, tape-record portions of Bill Steele's story (chap. 8) so that it sounds like a first-person account from the missionary himself. (HINT: It will sound more believable and add variety if someone other than you provides the voice. Choose someone who will read with energy and feeling.) Introduce the tape by telling participants they are going to hear about a part of the world that is in the news every night. Identify Bill Steele and his job, then play the tape.

Afterwards, ask each participant to name one thing that particularly moved them. How did it make them feel to hear that their world hunger offering was being used this way?

4. Using a flip chart or blackboard, ask participants to brainstorm responses to the words *public housing project*. After a few minutes, stop and see if there is a common thread among the responses, such as fear or avoidance. Tell the story of Terry Moncrief and Techwood housing project in Atlanta, Georgia. Emphasize that Techwood residents respond not just to the food they receive but to the respect and love shown them by the volunteers who distribute the food.

5. Tell participants that you have discovered a wonderful new food called a traroc [TRAY-rock]. It is from another country; and though no one in your area has ever grown, cooked, or eaten a traroc, everyone should start doing so immediately. It doesn't look or taste like anything they have ever experienced. They should eat them, even if they don't like the taste. Children should eat a traroc a day. Keep saying, "Just trust me. Trarocs are good for you."

You will probably get some good-humored resistance, and perhaps a few willing to try a traroc. This lighthearted discussion introduces the story of Sandy Johnson and the Ethiopian carrot patch (chap. 4). Point out that missionaries have to consider many cultural factors in nutrition and transformational work.

6. Using information from the book, make a matching game somewhat like Concentration. Place the squares on the wall or on the floor and divide participants into teams. Some possible matches are:

mendacity fatigue	burnout from constant giving
night blindness	stems from lack of vitamin A
Terry Moncrief	Techwood housing project
Beverly Goss	women's shelter
scurvy	stems from lack of vitamin C

Use information which you have covered in the study. You may wish to use one match from material which you have not covered. Call attention to that match and use it to introduce new material.

7. Read the quote from missionary Harold Watson (p. 74) concerning how much food America wastes. Discuss ways that food could be saved and shared with others.

8. Ask participants to move around the room reading quotes which you have displayed. Instruct them to write down a quote that best sums up their beliefs about hunger ministry. When all are seated, let a few volunteers read aloud his or her quote.

9. Bring up the research on hunger in your area. In light of what you have learned in the study, how could your church become servants to the hungry in your community? Your state? In America? The world? Draw the group beyond the usual responses of collecting and taking food to a shelter or giving money (though such ideas are good ones, and should also be done). Remind them of the creative approaches used by Augustine Salazar in California and Harold Watson and Jeff Palmer in the Philippines.

10. Remind participants of the scenarios you discussed in the beginning of the study. Would they change any of their responses? Do they have a better understanding of any of those situations?

Close the study by asking someone to read Luke 14:12-14. Remind them that just as the people featured in the study were servants of the banquet, so we are each called to be so. Emphasize that Christian hunger ministries differ from secular assistance because Christians seek to fill spiritual as well as physical hunger. Close in prayer.

Church Study Course Requirements

Servants of the Banquet is course number 03397 in the subject area Christian Growth and Service in the Church Study Course.

Credit for the course may be obtained in two ways: (1) conference or class; read the book and participate in a 2½-hour study; (2) individual study; read the book and write a brief summary of each chapter. (Have written work checked by an appropriate church leader.) Credit for this course may be applied to requirements for WMU Leadership Diploma.

Request credit on Form 725, "Church Study Course Enrollment/Credit Request," available from the Church Study Course Awards Office, 127 Ninth Avenue, North, Nashville, TN 37234.

Complete details about the Church Study Course system, courses available, and diplomas offered is in the *Church Study Course Catalog* available from the Awards Office.

About the author

Cathy Butler is a free-lance writer and a graduate of Southern Baptist Theological Seminary and the University of Alabama. She lives in Birmingham, Alabama, with her husband and son.

People in other parts of the world want to do better, but are at a disadvantage; and if we can't show them the love of Christ by sharing our abundance, we have no excuse for it. I don't think the excuses people make (for not helping the hungry) are going to count for much when we stand before our Maker."—Don Blasingame, former coordinator of Brotherhood Agricultural Fellowship